Stories That Need to Be Told

2017

Stories
That Need to Be Told 2017

edited by
Jennifer Top

TULIPTREE
PUBLISHING, LLC

CONTENTS

MARY'S STORY
OR, THE DAY KONY CAME
Georgia Baddley

This poem is dedicated to the women of Uganda
and the staff and volunteers of BeadforLife.

From Kampala we went
into the bush
off the main Orum road
deep into Otuke
in a safari van
on a narrow goat path

into the bush

to the tidy dirt compound
with huts of clay
and straw bricks
to meet Mary
to hear her story.

Sitting under a mango tree
Mary told her story
weariness draped like a shawl
pressing her down
fingers gripping her chair

Mary told her story

pain in her eyes
speaking resolutely of
unspeakable horrors
Mary told her story.

The day of her abduction
she hoed cassava
singing smiling
Anders in her belly
seven months
kicked hard

and Kony came

she couldn't flee
she walked too slow
her family there
she had to stay
and Kony came.

Kony's men
pillaged her family farm
beheaded her father-in-law
a gun pointed at her
seventy-kilo bag on her head
Mary forced to walk

the day Kony came

she saw her sister-in-law's body
she couldn't rest
resters macheted to death
Mary forced to walk

the day Kony came

she jumped a ditch

she couldn't fall
or the machetes would get her
on and on sixteen kilometers
the world's woes on her head
Mary forced to walk
the day Kony came.

Nightfall in camp
far from her family farm
more captives came
chaos and confusion

Mary fled

soldiers hunted her
in the blackness she hid
like a drum her heart
beat in fear

Mary fled

she ran and hid like a hare
through the night
for twenty kilometers
Mary fled
reaching safety in the refugee camp
the day after Kony came.

ANNOTATED LOVE LETTER

Alexander Joseph

Remember that day?[1] We drove down the dirt road[2] and we stopped by the river.[3] Things were simple then,[4] things were good, and life was the way I had always hoped it could be.

Well, I know that things aren't that way anymore[5] and I know that the spark and the heat that it once created (between us) has dulled. And I know that today, well this morning, is something special for you (and for me) and for us.[6] And this morning, in the dark, before I go to work, I am leaving you this note[7] and these flowers[8] and this thing in the box[9] that I have bought for you and I hope that it's enough.[10]

Yours,

Me.

p.s. There is no need to make or get dinner tonight, I've got it covered.[11]

---

[1] A day that was more cold than warm, if I remember correctly, and that was towards the end of November in the middle of a week (maybe a Wednesday) on a year in which November was not a month that had much snow at all but instead had a sort of low hanging (like an unwanted beer belly) fog cover that seemed to constantly and chillingly blow chokingly humid air onto the dirt roads that surrounded our house for not only most of November but also December and the beginning of January as well. And that day was special in some ways, as in I am sure it was somebody's birthday somewhere (or more likely many thousands of people's birthdays) but it was neither of our

birthdays, and it was not a holiday (at least not one that we were observing) but it was still special because we were together and even though we were so busy those days, every moment that we had free of work or sleep or whatever, we tried to spend together because those were the times, the minutes, the seconds, and dry-lipped kisses that kept us gong and doing those things we did so we could continue to survive together. And it was foggy out and it was an evening (or maybe later than that) in the middle of a week in which we were both working more than forty hours and that we both had to work at like 6 am the next day. And because of our early shifts in the morning, it was maybe a bit irresponsible for us to be out that night (well that day) in the fog and maybe we should've been at home winding down and getting ready to get a solid amount of sleep to be like fully rested and refreshed for the next day, but none of that really mattered and what did matter was the fact that were together and that we both would've happily stayed up all night together and would've had to slog through work the next day, but it would've been worth it to not sleep if we got to spend that time together, awake and warm, instead.

[2] And that dirt road was the place that we would always go when we were together, when we didn't have enough time or money to actually go any real places or do any real-life things, but those real things we could've done were always too expensive and reality was subjective anyway and we had more fun on that dirt road than at any of those other places anyway. And that day, that evening, that night, we drove in the fog down that dirt road in your old, teal car that squeaked and whistled as it coasted and hopped over potholes and puddles. And in that car, there were empty bags and bottles from snacks and drinks that we or you or me had had in the past and had thrown behind the front seats, and the back seats were folded down and covered with a blanket that was once black but now was gray with dog hair from your dog, but that day, that evening, that night in the fog, it had just been me and you. We left the dog at home because she was asleep under the kitchen table and had looked so cozy and warm and sort of innocent beneath that table, that we decided to let her stay asleep and we left in your teal car to go for a drive down our favorite road. And that evening the dog was back at home but there was a lot of dog hair and trash in the car and the tank was almost empty (the light was on, telling us we needed

to get gas) but we didn't care about any of that, we didn't care about the shambles, because we had each other, because I had your hand in both of mine and on the radio (even though the speakers were blown and the words were garbled almost beyond recognition) one of our favorite songs was playing (it was the one with the minor chords and the two singers).

[3] And that river was cold then, but wasn't completely frozen over yet. And the water was flowing fast that night and the fog was so low above the river that it looked like the river was kind of coming from the sky and the clouds, and I remember you said that to me as we were parked at a pull-off beside the river, that the river sort of followed the winding dirt road. And we had the windows up and the defrost in the car was on, but we were breathing too much maybe and the windows were fogged up anyway, so we got out of the car, even though we were not wearing enough clothes to keep us warm we still went outside. And we sat on the hood of the car and looked out at the river and didn't speak, and I put my arm around your shoulders and pulled you in close and you wrapped your arms around my chest and you wrapped one of your legs around mine (that way that I always told you drove me crazy, but in a good way) and you rested your head in the crook of my shoulder.

[4] And then you told me that you were in one of your favorite places, because I was keeping you warm and with one eye you could see my neck and my face and the stubble on both but with the other eye you could see the sky and the trees and with your ears you could hear the river and with your body you could feel my breathing and I could feel yours too. And your breath came out in a small cloud that matched the texture and color of the fog but smelled kind of like strawberries and I always wondered how you always smelled so good those days, even when you had eaten the same things as me. How did you always smell like strawberries, even in the morning when I would lean over and kiss you to wake you up, I could never understand that. Ever since I was a little kid, I imagined that adults just woke up and got to do whatever they wanted to do. I always imagined that adults everywhere, while I suffered in school, were just having fun. When I became an adult, I obviously realized that my previous outlook on adult life was not

correct and in fact that I had wasted my childhood hoping to have fun in adulthood when in reality it was the other way around. When we met (remember that night in the snow?) I was working and everything seemed muted; void of color; gray. Adulthood was a grind that seemed to never end and childhood's hopes were dashed and dead thanks to the grinding of machines and the bright white of office computer screens. But that night in the snow and the new life that has followed, has been what I hoped I could be. No matter what we're doing (whether it's waking up late and staying in bed reading and laughing or taking drives down our road or making dinner together or just sitting still and letting the rain soak us so wet that our clothes sag and droop and we have to cuddle to get warm and dry again) with you that dream of somehow doing just what I want has come true. What I am saying is that you are just what I want and what I need and what I have always wanted and what I have always needed, even if I don't say it as often as I should.

[5] I know that the days seem long and sometimes we are so quiet that the air between us seems cold and hard. I know that sometimes I don't say what I mean, and I know that sometimes you look at me in that way that only you can and I know that look means that you are considering us, as in me and you and if us two are meant to be together. And I know when it's snowing and the sun is hidden behind white and the wind sounds like a train whistle as it whips across the roof and work is still there but it's harder in the dark, I know that you want it to be easy to come home and I want that too and I know that sometimes it's not and it's a different but equally nasty kind of cold inside. And I want you to know I am sorry for that and I am sorry for the times you have smiled even though you were tired and that I didn't smile back. And I'm sorry for the times that you touched my back or kissed my neck and I pulled away, and it's not that I didn't want you to touch me (you know I always do or maybe you don't know, but I do) and I'm sorry for the coldness that I sometimes radiate.

[6] As in today is that day that we first met, but two years after.

[7] And as you can see, this note is written on the paper from that notebook that you got for me so I could try and practice my drawings

that you have always said are really promising. And I want you to know that I appreciate your support and your love and everything you have done for me and those days that you have worked longer than normal, as in a double or as in overtime, so that you could get some extra money to pay for these little presents that you always leave for me in the morning. And that is why this morning, before I leave for the day (a day that I wish I could spend with you) I am leaving some little presents around the house, like you have often done for me.

[8] And these flowers are the ones you said were pretty that night by the river under the stars. When we were lying on the hood and you looked down and pointed at these light purple flowers by the river and even though that was just the beginning, before we shared a bed every night and before we were an us, I remembered that you pointed out those flowers and last night (before you got home from work) I went back to that riverbank and I picked those flowers that you pointed out. And these flowers are sort of like us, they have had two years to bloom and grow, and even though they are older now and their color has faded a bit and their petals seem a bit rougher and more worn than before, they seem stronger and their roots are thicker. These two flowers that I picked are for you and me and they are also for us.

[9] And this thing in the box is a photograph that I had printed of me. It's that photo that you took that day after we had finally dried off after sitting in the rain and in the photo I am sitting with a towel around my neck and my hair is all over the place and I'm smiling this big, wide goofy smile that only you can make me do and I'm sort of looking at the camera (but I'm really looking at you). And I know it's not a necklace and I know it's not some fancy ring, this photo is me at my finest and my finest is when I am with you. And I have only become who I am today because of you and the warmth that comes with the smile that you and only you can make me wear and it has made me into something softer. Those calluses and those tightly drawn muscles in my chest that you always put your soft hands on; those hard parts of me; those things I have locked away; those tears I never cried because I was told I shouldn't; those muffled screams: you have melted me into something soft and warm like you and I am new because of it. Without those soft touches, without those whispers of love in the

night; without those drives to the river and those wide eyes that just cut me down, without all that I would be out in the cold. I would be that thing I thought I would never be. Without those eyes and that way that you listen when I need you to, I would be just some person who had grown up to a life of gray, of work, of blankness, the opposite of what I had always dreamed. And with this photograph in the box that I'm leaving with this note and those flowers that I picked just for you, I hope that you will keep it with you (somewhere safe and secret that only you know) and when you look at it I hope you will remember that I will try to be, always, what you have been to me, there, whenever you need.

[10] And I hope that I am enough.

[11] I'll be making that dish we had that night after we saw your parents and you were upset and I pulled the car over and stopped at the little place and you were too mad to talk and I kissed your hand and you gave me that look that you give (the scary one) but I knew you weren't mad at me and you eventually came around and you cried during the meal and you said (later) that that night you told me things that you had told nobody else and I know that was a hard night for you but it was one of the best nights for me because I was there for you and I could support you like you have always done so well for me. And I want to make you this meal that you said you enjoyed because I want you to know, that if you are down and on those days when our spark is dim or fading, that I will be there to kiss your hand and to be there, whenever you need.

BEATS

Jon Shorr

1

I'm walking on the treadmill, in step with "Mr. Tambourine Man" playing in my head, radioactive dye coursing through my arteries. The cardiologist is talking about the Orioles and the Ravens and his having gone to school with the University of Baltimore's new president. I'm not paying attention to him, partly because I haven't been following the Orioles and don't plan to follow the Ravens, and partly because I'm anticipating the pain from those little adhesive squares that are thinking of little else than looking forward to pulling the hair off 167 pieces of my body.

"Are you experiencing any chest pain?" the cardiologist asks between reciting Brian Matusz's pitching stats.

"No," I say, "other than anticipating those little pieces of tape pulling the hair off my chest."

"No, really," he says, "what level of pain are you experiencing right now?"

"None," I say, wishing there were something other than a blank wall to look at.

"You should be experiencing major pain right now," he says. "I have to tell you that your EKG is highly abnormal."

"In a good way or a bad way?" I ask, pretty sure of the answer.

"You know those marathon runners that drop dead of heart attacks and everyone says, 'But they were in perfect health!' They weren't in perfect health; they were just asymptomatic. That's you."

2

I don't usually read the fine print on all those waivers and disclaimers and permission forms you have to sign before medical people will even let you in the room, much less do whatever it is they're going to do to you. It's like reading the possible side effects of drugs, all of which you're sure you're going to get, or the 224 warning signs of some awful disease, most of which, you suddenly realize, you already have. Why would you do that to yourself! But here I am sitting on the side of the bed in the little pre-op cubicle, holding my open-back gown shut, waiting to be wheeled to wherever for the cardiac catheterization so the doctors can confirm that the "highly abnormal" EKG was caused by some arterial blockages, realizing I've already read that issue of *People* magazine in some other holding pen while waiting for some other doctor. "This procedure," the form begins, "could produce various collateral effects, including bruising at the incision site, infection, problems with heart rhythm, perforated blood vessels, kidney damage, heart attack, stroke, death, and allergic reaction." It's bad enough that I might end up with kidney failure or a perforated artery or even dead, I think, reading about the increasing severity of the unintended consequences, but I sure hope I don't have an allergic reaction.

3

Three days later I say goodbye to my wife and kids. They wheel me through hallways and elevators to a corridor outside the operating room. "See you in a couple hours," I'd said, hoping it was true.

People in scrubs wander past. The anesthesiologist gives me more forms to sign. "We'll give you a shot to help you relax," she says. "Then we'll move you onto the operating table and put you under. We'll put a breathing tube down your throat and a catheter through a vein in your neck so we can monitor heart pressures during the procedure. We'll insert drainage tubes in your chest and add a second IV line in your arm, as well as a line to monitor your blood pressure." She lists other tubes and wires. "Then the surgeons will saw through your sternum and begin the operation," she says, "during which time they'll remove veins from your leg and your chest wall to bypass your blocked arteries. They'll replace your aortic valve with one made of cow tissue and connect you to a heart-lung machine to keep your blood and oxygen flowing while your heart's stopped."

I want my mommy.

"One thing, though," she says at the end. "In order for the anesthesia mask to fit securely, we may have to trim your beard. Would that be okay?"

4

It's like a dream, but it's not. I'm in the Cardiac Intensive Care Unit, the CICU, for the first couple days after surgery. There's no privacy, not that I care; the staff can see us constantly through the glass walls and sliding glass doors that separate the rooms from the nurses' station. I'm lying there, still somewhat drugged, when a light starts flashing in the hall. Several people in green scrubs and Flintstones smocks run to the room across the hall. The light keeps flashing. More people rush in. I doze off. I wake up and see two people in scrubs, outside my room, hugging. Others are just milling about in the hallway, some blotting their eyes and wiping their noses with tissues. The room across the hall is empty: the bed's gone; the IV poles and monitors are gone. It's just an empty space. I doze off. Three men in khakis and knit shirts are in the room, writing occasionally on their clipboards, talking with a man in a suit. I ask the tech who comes in what happened across the hall.

"Nothing," she says, checking my vital signs, her eyes red.

"What are those guys doing there?" I ask.

"They're just conducting a routine inspection," she says.

"Where's the person that was in that room?" I ask.

"They moved him," she says.

5

I'm on the "step-down" ward, the place they park you when you don't need to be in the CICU any longer. And I'm off the post-op morphine drip, too, just taking some extra-strength Tylenol for pain. Of course, they have me on 30 or so other drugs, and the side effects from some of those, as well as the machines' constant beeping and tooting, as well as the 24-hour light in the room and the hallway, as well as the nurses and techs coming by every 12 or so minutes to check my temperature or blood pressure or take some blood or offer me some water or ask how I'm feeling or ask if I'm able to sleep make it virtually impossible to sleep. On the advice of a person who's spent a lot of time in hospitals, my wife buys me a sleep mask, hoping that it might help even a little. Although I'm mildly concerned about being mistaken for either Arlene Francis from *What's My Line?* or the Lone Ranger, I try it on, just as the efficient Pakistani nurse enters the room to check my vitals.

"Is that you, Tonto?" I ask in my best post-op Clayton Moore voice.

And the nurse, who has no 1950s or '60s American pop culture referents, asks, concerned, "Mr. Shorr, are you hallucinating?"

6

The hospital food is better than I expected. Rather than getting the generic tray of thin gruel, which I expect, I can phone in my order from a respectable-looking "room service" menu. I'm somewhat surprised not only that the room service phone answerer will only let me order "heart healthy" items (how does she know that I'm recovering from heart surgery and not a broken tibia?), but that she kept track of my earlier orders, so when I ordered low-fat cheese on my turkey sandwich on wheat, she reminded me that because I'd gotten pudding with my lunch, I'd maxed out on fat for the day. The whole heart-healthy diet thing continues to baffle me. Can I really have more salt if it's sea salt? Is lean organic beef really better for me than extra lean inorganic bison? Nevertheless, when my friend Danny and I go to breakfast at Suburban House months later, and he gets the lox and whitefish salad and bagel and cream cheese platter, I make do with a mushroom and spinach egg white omelet, a fruit cup instead of home fries. And at Kooper's North, I covet his bacon cheeseburger ("bleu cheese, please, extra mayo and hot sauce"), accompanied by duck fat fries and cole slaw, while I pick at my dry turkey sandwich and garden salad with oil and vinegar dressing.

7

They come from miles around, it seems. "It's so straight!" the residents say. "It's so small!" the physicians' assistants say. "They're usually twice that long . . ." I realize they're talking about my incision and relax. ". . . and jagged," the home-care nurses say. Sometimes I feel like they're more interested in visiting my incision than visiting me. My incision needs its own visiting hours, its own private room. The bruise, on the other hand, is on the other hand, the one most battered by the IV. But it's nothing like the Big Bruise, the one that might've made me a black-and-blue ribbon winner at the state fair, had there been a competition for post-op bruises. It doesn't show up 'til the day after I get home. It starts on my right side and wraps halfway around my back, making me look like I'm decked out for Ravens Friday in Baltimore.

"Holy shit," the visiting nurse lets slip when she comes by the next day to check me out, "that's quite a bruise!"

"Does it mean something's wrong?" I ask, still clueless about which post-op recovery symptoms are normal and which are abnormal.

"Nah, it's fine," she says. "You probably just slept at a funny angle. That anticoagulant they put you on can do some crazy stuff. Don't worry; you won't bleed to death. It'll go away eventually."

8

The music ranges from "Let's Twist Again Like We Did Last Summer" and "Wake Up, Little Susie" to "Shout" and "Hello, Mary Lou (Goodbye, Heart)." The outlier is the *Rocky* theme, celebrating somebody's graduation from cardiac rehab. My class consists of men, white, of an age, graying and in most cases balding, several with noticeable paunches. A couple have new stents, a couple are recovering from heart attacks, a couple from bypasses or valve replacements, and a couple have had various combinations of those.

Before I can get onto the treadmill, I have to sign a form acknowledging that I know how to use the machine, agree not to misuse it, and release the hospital, staff, manufacturer, and my third-grade gym teacher from any responsibility should I hurt myself or those around me. Same thing before I get on the bike and sometime later when I advance to the rower. Finally, there's the form acknowledging that if the blinds are open, people outside might be able to see me exercising. I still don't know if this is about HIPAA privacy rights or a response to a complaint from someone (inside? outside?). Given the way several of us look in our workout clothes, it seems appropriate that passersby should also have to sign a form releasing the hospital from responsibility for grossing them out.

9

It's the fifth week of cardiac rehab; I've just hooked myself up to the wireless heart monitor and am getting ready to do my stretches. "Jon, come over here and sit down; we need to talk," one of the nurses calls out to me. What she needs to talk to me about is my heartbeat, which is 160 and looking more like Morse code than clockwork. "You're in a-fib," she says. "Do you know what that is?"

I know exactly what it is. It had kicked in once before, a couple days after surgery, and took about a month for my heart to settle into a normal (sinus) rhythm. "It's fairly common after valve replacements," the cardiologist had said. "Your heart's been traumatized, and often, it not only takes the parts time to relearn their jobs but learn· how to work together again." Now, two months later, it's back. They bring in a wheelchair and wheel me to the ER ("You don't need to do this" I say; "I can walk").

"We're going to give you a shot," the ER nurse says. "It might solve the problem, but usually it doesn't, in which case we'll have to admit you."

It doesn't. They do. By that afternoon it is mostly back to normal. They keep me overnight and send me home the next morning.

10

Every Monday night when I was little, I emptied onto the bed the carton of Camels that my dad brought home and then put them in the empty drawer of his bedside table, sometimes lining them up, sometimes alternating them right side up and upside down, sometimes laying them down and stacking them, sometimes lining them up in military columns. I liked loading pennies into wrappers, too, 50 at a time, then trying to build a penny-wrapper pyramid without their rolling all over the table.

Now, every Sunday night, I load a week's worth of pills into one of those multisectioned pill boxes that I used to see on my grandfather's kitchen table: lisinopril and metoprolol for blood pressure, pravastatin for cholesterol, amiodarone to slow my heartbeat, Eliquis to reduce clotting. And there's the stuff the doctors don't seem to care about: vitamins C and D, a multivitamin, and some fish oil/omega-3. My blood pressure wasn't that high to begin with, nor was my cholesterol that bad. And frankly, who cared if my heartbeat wasn't Greenwich-Atomic-Clock regular? Now, though, all those things seem to matter.

I dump several pills from each bottle onto the kitchen counter and arrange them in the daily pill compartments, sometimes the big ones on the bottom, sometimes one atop the other, and then drop the little ones around them.

11

I'm a drummer; I've been one since fifth grade. I'm one of the snare drummers the band director looked to to keep a steady 140 beat as the Mt. Healthy High School band marched briskly down the hill and onto the field to play "The Star Spangled Banner" before the game. I'm the bass drummer the Miami University band relied on to keep the tempo steady during "Edelweiss" in "The Sound of Music" medley. I'm the timpanist that helped hold disparate parts together during the Hamilton Symphony Orchestra's performance of Borodin's Second Symphony. I'm the guy in the Golden Touch Quartet that kept the sax and piano on target during their "Green Dolphin Street" riffs. What is a drummer, after all, if not someone who can keep a steady beat? What good is a drummer who can't keep a steady beat? Being a drummer is one of the ways I've always defined myself. I was the guy they could literally count on. Now, between the a-fib, the atrial tachycardia, and the other random arrhythmias that I've probably always had but that no one ever said were particular problems, my heart periodically sounds more like a scat duet between Louis Armstrong and Ella Fitzgerald than "The National Emblem March." How can I call myself a drummer? And if I'm not a drummer, what am I?

12

"Are you hurt, sir?" the 12-year-old trainer asks. I'd fallen off the treadmill.

"I'm fine," I say, standing up, resuming my exercise, staring at my wrist.

I'm a counter; I look for patterns. I may lean a bit toward OCD or Asperger's. I like to measure random distances—elbow to nose, shirt pocket to eyebrow. Walking home from junior high, I counted the steps from Steve Shipp's house to mine. Sometimes I count the steps from my office to my car. I enjoyed counting the rests in symphonic music between snare drum rolls or triangle dings. I live for "12:34" and "11:11" on digital clocks. One time, I drove across town after my wife called to say she'd pulled to the side of the road because she knew I'd want to see the odometer roll over to 100,000 miles.

Now at the gym I wear a heart rate monitor, which I watch. Constantly.

Watching it exacerbates my terrible balance. It also plays havoc with my treadmill television watching: one minute, Cary Grant and his submarine crew are dodging depth charges; the next, they're passing under the Golden Gate Bridge; I have no idea what happened in between because I'm so busy trying not to fall off again while looking at my wrist: 62, 62, 84, 65, 57, 91, 61.

13

I'd read about the paranoia, the "post-event depression" in heart patients but figured I'd missed it: I'm reasonably healthy, and reasonably rational; I understand the process, recovery time line, and risks. And I've always thought of myself as a fatalist, a realist: *que sera sera*. Yet every twinge in my shoulder, arm, chest says, "Here comes The Big One"; every twinge in my head, every slow focus shift becomes the precursor to the stroke that's going to leave me in a vegetative state, drain my savings, and make caregivers of my wife and children. In fact, I'm probably reasonably okay, except for the alfalfa cravings, the result, I'm sure, of the cow-tissue replacement valve. I also know that I am no longer, as Tennyson said, "that strength which moved earth and heaven."

My acupuncturist likens bodies to geographic masses, across which weather systems move. Sometimes it's cloudy; the clouds pass. Sometimes there are snow showers or wind gusts. Sometimes there are tornadoes or hurricanes. Sometimes, afterward, there's debris to clean up; there are parts that need to be fixed or rebuilt.

I could just think of it as yet another little blip on that gradual, downward slide toward death.

Right now, though, I need to figure out how I'm going to focus the *La La Land* discussion tomorrow in my film class.

My grandfather died of a stroke when he was younger than I am.

I need to get to the Sherwin Williams store to buy the supplies for repainting our downstairs ceilings this weekend.

My dad's two siblings died of heart attacks when they were younger than I am.

I need to leave in an hour for my granddaughter's middle school orchestra concert.

My dad died of a heart attack. He was older than I am.

No Superhero

Lisa Poff

There was a white moth
with brown polka dots
flying in the shower
while I was bathing
my daughter.
It was young like her,
and it started to flutter
right where the water
might hit its wings.

The moth was struck
by a single drop,
(a tsunami to a bug)
and fell in a puddle.
The dots became
a brown powder,
surrounding it
like a cape in the water.

I felt that I could save it
with a bit of toilet paper.
So I threw in that dry lifeline
and it clung with tiny might,
until it let go and flew to
the safest place it could find—
straight down the drain.

I cried for its soaking wet,
broken wings,
but I was really crying
for everything.
If I could have fixed
this miniscule hurt,
then we would surely
save the world.

LE CHÂTEAU POSSONNIERE

Mario René Padilla

> A kiss makes the heart young again
> and blows away the years.
> —Rupert Brooke

Sofie and I arrived at her cousin's château, road tired and hot, backs sweaty, shirts sticking to the seats. A kiss and an impulsive embrace, we barely made it out of the car. The whole drive she spoke of love, non-stop it seemed, but it was ours she desperately wanted to plumb. My unannounced, extended visit was test enough of our time together in L.A.—were those seven months just a passing infatuation?

"You came to me, sweetie. I knew you can't forget me. Ma rose est de plus en plus belle chaque jour."

Being with a poet meant constantly explicating her verse. She was always reciting Verlaine or Rimbaud or some other French symbolist—poets I too loved and was writing about in my thesis when we met.

"Tu comprends ce que je veux dire, no? En France, age differences mean nothing."

I remained quiet, for the comment had the opposite effect of her intent. Age. An un-erasable fact. Always on us like skin. I missed being young in love's hope and naïve to le terrible of life. I thought of our twenty years' difference, twenty more summers I'd seen than Sofie.

She drove, speaking passionately of Rimbaud, how his great verse came so young, then nothing. Done by the age of twenty-one—indifferent to the transitory quality of time as only the young can be. She mentioned my great promise as a writer, and I thought about Rimbaud dying at the age of 37 with one leg as I looked out the window at the iconic French countryside passing in stages of late

August harvest, the sunflowers beginning to wilt, the large rolls of hay in the fallow-reaped fields—end of season. I listened quietly to her express how good life can be for artists in France, and, whenever appropriate, smiled, reciting lines I still remembered of Rimbaud for good measure, joking about her touring skills, about keeping her eyes on the road because I was too young to die, all the time knowing I'd booked a flight to L.A. end of August.

We'd driven north out of Paris toward Angers early that morning after *un petit déjeuner*, lattés and croissants at a sidewalk table of her favorite boulangerie, the charming sounds of the Left Bank just waking up to the heat and crescendo of life. Renoir could have painted her in that scene, her profile at that breakfast table so lovely in the new sun, leaning forward on her elbows, sitting before a brilliant white table cloth, her straw hat with flowers on the brim cocked to one side over her light brown curls, her delicate fingers spreading marmalade with the back of a silver demitasse spoon, sliced brie on fine ceramic plates with royal blue rimmed decoration, and the large bouquet of flowers I'd surprised her with the night before blossoming in a vase on the table. She refused to leave them to wilt *uncommended* in her Paris apartment, acting as if she'd never received such a bouquet of flowers before. She purposely wore my favorite outfit, because today was important to her: a white muslin blouse, a sky blue skirt with a red cloth belt bow-tied in the back—yes, she *was* a Renoir, a poster child for a travel advertisement that might have read *Come to France where all twenty-something girls are beautiful with flakes of croissant on their faces looking as if they are sitting for Renoir.*

That's what I was thinking when she suddenly said, "You seem far away, sweetie. Have you already left me, ma grenouille?"

Did she know? No, she couldn't have, though she was intuitive that way. "Mais non. Not far, mon lapin. Just love hearing you talk, that's all. I'm looking forward to meeting your cousin."

I had agreed to go with her to La Possonnierre to meet her cousin, Le Comte de la Possonnierre. He was dying, and one of three family members she had left in her life, which included an estranged sister in Australia with whom she rarely spoke and her mother in Tornus. But why? Why did she have such faith in me—believed I had come to stay, and on so little evidence other than our short time together in L.A.? Why did she believe so firmly that I was the one? The *one*—oh, the responsibility in that expression, to be the one somebody wanted for life. It wasn't that I was incapable of falling in love and being the *one* for someone again . . . and it wasn't that I hadn't fallen in love with her already, at least love as I'd come to understand it. How could I not? She was so full of qualities that dipped a lost soul back into life. Like her, I too once brimmed with verse, embraced life's possibilities, until I became familiar with love's Janus face, the yellow, narrow eyes—the Joker's grin.

We spoke French, except when we switched to English for threads of conversation too important for misunderstanding. Arriving at La Possonniere, she filled in another important detail she'd chosen so far to leave out: how she'd lost her father young, and this cousin, her royal cousin, the last of her line, stepped into his place. And "oh Christ," I thought. I was meeting her father.

"You see, he never lies to me. And I'm always honest with him. That's why we are such friends. But he lives so alone in life, no wife, no children—so alone, to die like that is sad, no?"

That made me uncomfortable, as if my own Janus face might be exposed by her close ally. Would he spy some evidence of my confusion, my troubled heart, my tired dreams leaking through the smile on my other face—writer of a slim volume of poems, a few published stories, an incomprehensible novel, nothing else to speak of really, mostly because I waste so much time writing commercial copy for an advertising agency. There's health insurance, car payments, and always the rent. And now my M.A. tuition, because I decided to go back to school and get an English degree to teach the written word full-time—stop being my own burden. Would her cousin detect all this, look at me and think, *forty-three, huh? Well, he who can, does. He who cannot, teaches.*

When Sofie and I met last November she thought me younger. We met at a friend's house in Santa Monica, sitting outside in his candlelit garden. He'd called me to come and meet his friend from France because I too was a poet and spoke French. In no time at all, we were spending time together. We knew we wanted each other from the moment we met. We walked Venice Beach, stood before paintings at LACMA, sat long hours in cafés where I'd often write—sitting together at an intimate table, as she added pages to her dissertation on overpopulation in large cities and the impact on the oceans. Whenever

I asked, she'd read my stories, and with a critically astute and concise comment, improve them. Then we'd return to my apartment, make love at night as only French women know how, I presume, for I'd never known any lover like Sofie, someone who treated being in love like an art form.

She bought me a planter, a ceramic reclining frog with forget-me-nots blossoming over the edge, saying, "Ma grenouille, si tu savais a quell point tu me manques when you and I are not together." So, she moved into my apartment for the last three months of her student visa for dissertation research, filling me up almost every night with her passion for love, her lust for intimacy. I found myself writing poetry again, dreaming in French. She was the only woman who had ever jumped into my arms when we saw each other. So, yes, that kind of affection has its effect. How could it not? I learned from her how to do and say everything that would make our time more intimate—an old dog with a too late new trick I guess—making love whenever she wanted, which seemed like all the time. I even bought her a rabbit vase with forget-me-nots hanging over the edge. Yes, for that reason! But also because it seemed charming to say *mon lapin* in response.

"Ma grenouille, quand nous serons grands, nous habiterons tous les quatres dans une jolie maison avec les chevaux."

"Je crois, mon lapin," I'd joke back. "When we get older, toi et moi serons trés hereux en France, in our little country house with horses, and me in my wheelchair."

Now, why did I say that? Was I just practicing my French—or being French? I had no intentions of living out my life in France. Was loving in the French manner like an infusion, a virus one caught in constant contact? In Paris, I found myself in certain unguarded moments actually believing in *us*, walking hand in hand along the Seine, kissing on a bench in the Tullieries, a scene that always seemed scored by Satie. Could I really consider life here a possibility—but as quickly as the thought materialized, I'd wipe it away, thinking, "Just live in the moment, Mauro. For the now. What the hell is wrong with you?" as if some invisible chain had me fettered to California's coast and the clogged traffic on the 405.

Buying a ticket for Paris was an impulsive act. It made me feel, for one brief, unexplainable moment, spontaneously romantic again—to fly straight into the face of fact and reason. I remember the day. I was buried under June gloom, having just finished the last of my master's exams. I'd woken sweaty, in twisted sheets, went to my computer but couldn't write a word. I wanted nothing more than to be in Sofie's arms again, away from routine, syllabi, the ocean, traffic. The evidence all about me of my many failures, each one standing at attention like sentries on familiar street corners, in favorite shops and restaurants, the beaches where my ex-wife and I once played, loved, grew up together really, though it took me till my late twenties to find her. All those moments I wish I could get back and redo, the times I treated her like a sulking, discontented boy, when I began to feel like I was missing out on something greater *out there*. We kept putting off having children, always thinking "maybe next year," until at 37, we both knew it was done.

But love Sofie-style, garlanded in capricious whimsy, was that what love was really supposed to feel like? Alone in bed on a gray morning I suddenly needed to see her. So, I called a travel agent and in ten minutes it was done. Charming, spontaneous, poetic. I even quit my job, saw myself for a time—a writer in that fabled city for writers with a lovely French girl on my arm—all the time hoping, with her for a while, I could steal back some time.

Exiting at Possonniere, she turned off the main road onto her cousin's long estate drive. "Ma grenouille, I don't remember if I mention it," she said. "Don't say anything of his health. He is sensitive about his condition."

Condition? I thought. The "old boy" was five years older than me and already dying? And penniless. "Of course I won't. We'll just talk about the French Revolution. How I support the destruction of *noblesse oblige*."

Sofie fake frowned, hitting me on the arm. "Connard. Don't be so cruel."

"Hey, that kinda hurt."

"Well, you deserve it," she added with a fake pout.

"Look, I know how to talk to royalty. You just tell them everything they want to hear, and never disagree."

"Non lui pas. Not his *kind*. He's sensitive. He knows when people lie to him or worse, humor him."

I imagined she meant the dying kind.

"So he's a real comte or a vicomte or some such thing?"

"En fait, le dernier Comte de la Possonniere."

Bouncing along his estate drive, hitting when not dodging dozens of unfixed potholes, I thought how ominous that sounded—the *last* count, hell, the *last* anything really, with all the finality of things going on inside of me, feeling the coming of certain ends—while the boy inside my head kept playacting his role, make believing I was young again. Jesus, what middle-ager wouldn't strike a deal with devils or angels: absolutely give up his hard-earned wisdom for one more year of romance as a 23-year-old, buoyant and free?

"But to quit your job? That's a mistake. These jobs are hard to find," my cubicle buddy commented as I was cleaning out my desk. "And for such a young girl? That's flat-out *reckless*, man."

I corrected him, saying, "Nope, just plain ol' being irrational for once. That's what it is. Isn't love grand?"

Of course, playacting with Sofie had me seven rounds into a sparring match I was fated to lose. This I knew. But I was punch drunk with the word *love* snapping its knuckles toward my face, willing to take the blows, just to get in close with her one more time, for one more embrace.

The road to the château seemed to go on forever. At one point, it tunneled into a tree-lined canopy, like an enchanted forest, when Sofie stopped the car and said, "Regarde! Le voilá. See it?" Yes, I did. I was taken back. In the clearing at the end of the road, between the trees and up on a hill, sat the château, like something out of Poe's *House of Usher*. It was three stories and impressive. Yet, as we began to pull closer, I could see it was worn down by centuries. I felt a tug in my gut, though not of anticipated pleasure. More like caution, as if the place might be haunted. Or perhaps it was simply the pangs of hunger in my belly, for it had been three hours since we left Paris. Sofie indicated that her cousin still had a cook, who made authentic ratatouille that "one should die for."

"You mean 'to die for.'"

"Oh dis moi, mon professeur, my teacher of English."

Her half French, half English charmed me most I think. And it seemed that, as we arrived, we crossed over into some antique time when I should be speaking only French. Especially when we passed under the rust-corroded 20-foot ornate iron gate, rolling slowly over the cobblestones, up to the château's crumbling façade overlooking an impressive courtyard with dozens of dry, empty gardens full of weeds. The château, I understood from Sofie, had been built three and a half centuries ago as a vacation house by the original Comte du Romain for his young, beautiful contessa and regularly welcomed old powder-faced nobles with silk coats, white hose, and walking canes, with their servants and footmen guiding gilded two-horse carriages—young lovers behind curtained windows for dangerous liaisons.

Sitting in the car before the massive rustic wooden door, I reached for her and we kissed, and, at that moment, all I really wanted was to make love to her on the seats.

"On y va," she said, pulling away, straightening herself out.

Stepping from the car, she began dialing her cousin's number. Meanwhile, I took in the grounds. "Ah Bernard, c'est moi, nous sommes arrives . . ." They spoke as if overjoyed to be speaking to one another, though he was less than one hundred feet away from seeing her in person. I paced the paving stones, imagining all the carriages that once pulled up this same drive, on to this same courtyard with flowers in all the gardens, arriving for some masked ball or a concert by Chopin, the young genius sitting at a Steinway in the grand music room. But then, everything I saw killed that vibe. There were roof slates broken on the ground, the walls peeling layers of paint, a faded mauve under white, once pink, with broken shutters that hung askew, like an old man's drooping eyelids. The multi-paned windows, grimy in their disrepair, appeared like broken teeth in that same old man's face, no flowers, no manicured hedges—only idle weeds and aimless ivy climbing up the gutters, strangling the large waterless fountain that no longer remembered having trembled. In the dilapidated stable around the side of the château, what once might have held ten horses now had one aging horse lumbering to an empty trough, its unused tack hanging over a white fence turned beige by the sun. The whole house, now a mere specter of its youthful 17th century elegance, seemed to want us to depart. But we were here, and the plan was to stay the weekend.

"Jesus, I would have loved to have seen this place in its heyday, when the first Comte du Romain built it for his young contessa." Bowing from the waist, I grabbed her hand, kissing her knuckles. "May I escort you into the ballroom, my lady, or perhaps the bedroom?"

Smiling, Sofie played along. "Mais oui, monsieur," and she curtsied as I moved in for a kiss.

"But I must inform you," she said, breaking away, "the thirteenth is coming out any moment now."

At dinner, Bernard hardly said a word. And when he did talk, it was always prompted by a question from Sofie. Living alone as he did, sick and without friends, left him little energy and no use for social graces. He seemed to be speaking already from the bottom of a tomb. Strange how this specimen would be the end of the family's royal lineage. They spoke exclusively in French. He seemed to accept my presence though, as I quietly ate my ratatouille inside my sense of anonymity. I felt, for some reason, ham-fisted with the French language—certainly less fluent with the comte than with Sofie, and so, rarely joined in the conversation. He made me uncomfortable, not because of anything he said or any presumed dislike, but simply because he seemed already a ghost in a ghost house, and something I identified with disturbed me to the core. Hearing that I was a writer, he didn't bother to ask what I wrote.

"Sofie tells me you write for a living."

"Yes," I said, taking a sip of wine.

I thought it best not to say what exactly I wrote, for Sofie must have mentioned I wrote fiction and poetry.

Then they resumed their conversation; he glanced at me from time to time. Sofie spoke of finishing her dissertation, about her opportunity after graduating to work for Greenpeace at their Paris office on Rue d'Enghien. Bernard seemed pleased. His young cousin so ambitious, so capable of taking care of herself, relieved. Then he looked at me, and I thought I could hear him musing, *will she need to take care of him too?* So, I pulled up inside myself, looked at Sofie smiling, and wondered what the hell I was doing here. Why did she love me so much? Me? She could have any younger man she desired, and I felt the comte knew as much. Then I remembered my booked flight, and I found myself memorizing her tone of voice, how she said things. Like a newspaper reporter, I began burning into memory her face, her affectations as she sat laughing and entertaining her cousin in his last days. I wanted to imbibe her smile and compassionate eyes, which I knew I would need someday in L.A. Of course, old Bernard knew more about the fleeting nature of time than I, what it can do to the body, but that conversation was off limits. What was certain, he didn't know love's revenge like I did, four years removed from a marriage that was supposed to last. I had little time to waste on futile pursuits, but here I was in France, when a teaching job had to be found in L.A. There was nothing I could do in Paris but write and ride the horse she kept in Tornus. *Nothing I could do but write and be in love in Paris.* Jesus Christ, I was beginning to hate myself, the conventional parameters I'd constructed around my life.

"I should like to ask you something, Monsieur Mauro." Oh no. Here it comes. He was going to flush me out. "Sylvie tells me, besides stories and poetry, you are a commercial writer. Nonfiction I guess you call it."

"Yes. I'll write pretty much anything if there's a check in it." He didn't laugh, so I stopped short.

"I was wondering, would you consider writing a history of this house, something I cannot do, though I could tell you everything you need to know?" the comte suddenly said in perfect English.

"It has a fascinating history this house," Sofie added, as if there might be some doubt in my mind.

"I imagine it has a great story to tell," I said, thankful they weren't speaking French. *Unfortunately, I'm flying home in a week and a half* is what I should have said. "But I'm not sure I'm the writer for the job. What about Sofie? She's a wonderful writer. She'd be so much more emotionally connected I think."

"Sofie knows much, yes, but she's young." And his expression spoke volumes, not all of which I understood. "You, my good sir, seem a man experienced with life and love's intrigue, as well as its despair, I suspect. As they say, if this house could only speak. But it cannot. So, someone with experience and age must speak for it, while it is still remembered."

"Well . . . sure, I'd consider giving it a shot," I said with a crooked smile.

"Marvelous. Let's toast on it."

We grabbed our wine glasses and clinked.

The man spoke better English than I did, clearly schooled in England by his choice of words and accent. But just when the comte began to reveal his first secret about the house, which had been guarded for centuries, he suddenly apologized, stood up, and said, "Forgive me, but I must retire. I'm afraid I'm not a very good host tonight."

Sofie told him in French, "Don't be ridiculous." She insisted that he was always a great host and that we understood and would talk some more tomorrow.

As we said our good nights, his cook, Marie, came in from the kitchen and took his arm as he stood up. At the bottom of the stairs she turned and told Sofie which room she had prepared for us, then they disappeared up the long flight of stairs. Maybe it was the house's reputation, or the secret he would not be telling us, but I found myself wondering where Marie slept, for she never came back down.

With the house quiet, we took a bottle of Pernod and two apéritif glasses and climbed to our third-floor suite. The strong liqueur seeped into our veins. Wasting no time, we pulled back the burgundy bed cover, stripped, and crawled into bed, lost in each other's belief in our future together, like only Pernod could make us. We made love on silk monogrammed sheets, and as always, whenever we lay together, we slipped easily into passion that hands and mouths instinctively comprehend. The mahogany Louis XIV that framed our thrusting figures creaked so badly I thought we might have to move to the floor.

Afterward, we lay quietly intertwined in stale darkness and decay, in the scent of dust and the odor of cat feces from the many that roamed the place. I stroked Sofie's face and body, illuminated by faint slivers of moonlight that had slipped through the cracks in the shutters. She remained quiet until she said in low melancholic tones, "He's the last of our line you know—the last male of a family that was once, how should I say . . . vibrant. Est-ce que tu me comprends?"

"It means the same in English. But what about you? You're vibrant."

"Yes, but, you understand me, no? The line is dead."

And once again, all I wanted was to comfort her as she did me whenever I turned dark. Could I possibly change my plans and stay a while longer—forever?—with this creature of my subconscious? I knew, being from a different era, I would eventually become her burden. I should know better than to have flown back into her life, just when it was about to start. Always thinking of myself first, I guess. A terrible habit that had already cost me. Love for her should come easier, and much younger. Love for me was like the vampire bats that fluttered outside our window.

"Jesus, are those bats?" And once again Poe sprang to mind.

"Mon dieu," she said, got up, and ensured the shutters were latched, so many of the panes being broken. I grew quiet and listened to the clicking of the bats.

Knowing full well my heart's habit of growing meditative after orgasm, Sofie pulled my face into her moist breasts, breathing, "Je t'aime, je t'aime," thrusting herself against me, wanting my lips again, whispering in sultry French her ambitious plan to make life mythical again—as she guessed it must have been for me, once, when I was young.

Naturally, I'm a fool for melancholy love. So she grabbed a book from her purse and began to read to me, by lamplight, Verlaine's "La Chanson des Ingénues": of fresh skin maidens dancing their azure dreams, prancing through sunflower fields chasing butterflies. She read so beautifully that I could hear the wild thumping of their innocent hearts! And I knew this was not the time to tell her. I could not hurt her, not here, in her family's remnant. So we made love again, until we fell asleep.

Opening my eyes to sunrays piercing the shutter cracks where moonlight had been, Sofie rolled over toward me with sleepy eyes, yawning. She laughed as I told her my story of how I survived the long exhausting night, waking up a couple of times to take a pee (more and more frequently it seems). Saying how at first I was afraid to get out of bed, to walk through le comte's wretched house fearing the old contessa's ghost would step from her portrait hanging right above the bathroom door in the haunted hall.

"I imagined her cackling, hysterically, wagging her finger at me."

"Legend has it," Sofie whispered, "that whenever false lovers are discovered, she drags them from their beds and beheads them."

How endearing her accent, her smile, her sense of humor in the telling. And at that moment, nobody seemed more tuned in to my own peculiar nature.

"I hardly got any sleep," I complained.

"My poor sweetie. Quel dommage, ma grenouille."

And there it was again, her *infallible* dream of love—the one I'd learned always fails—how solid it felt to me now, like those dreams one wakes from but doesn't know he's still dreaming. And why not, after all? My feelings for her were honest, my embrace, earnest, and yes, I'd stay with her if I could, her brown hair tousled and splayed out across the pillow, to embrace the hope she still held in her comforting hands, the certainty that anyone could fall in love again—with the right person.

Jumping from the bed like a fresh skin maiden, Sofie opened the shutters, allowing the air and full sun to rush in, singing, "Let's ride bicycles into Possonniere!"

Winding through country roads, a baguette, bottle of wine, and a blanket in her basket, Sofie raised her arms, balancing herself like a circus act—agile and self-assured. Following in her wake, I too carefully lifted my hands from the bars, gingerly at first, unused to such fanciful tricks—a young man again testing his limits—as rows upon rows of wilting sunflowers lifted their withering seeds, one last time, toward the August sun.

RUN AMOK
Laura Eddy

On most Fridays, the Fresh Chef meal-kit box settled in on the front porch, like a contented cat, until Pete, or occasionally Greta, arrived home and hoisted it inside. Its insides of individually wrapped seasonal vegetables, paper-wrapped farm-fed meat, and crates of single eggs were then organized in the refrigerator like a small-scale Whole Foods. But this Friday, Pete arrived home to an empty porch. No cheerful red and latte-colored box to usher in the weekend.

That's annoying, he thought. Pete had planned to prepare one of the meals that night, cook one the next day to help feed Greta's sister and brother-in-law, and save the other as a weekday treat for Greta when she arrived home late from her job in the city. Now he would have to go shopping.

He entered the one-bedroom, two-story townhouse that he and Greta rented at a bargain price, at least by the small California college town's standards. After feeding Chia, their orange tabby cat, and filling up a mason jar with ice water, Pete flopped on the sofa. The sofa, an imitation midcentury piece from West Elm, had stretched their budget, but it was adult, though less so now that Chia had torn hundreds of small lacerations in its chenille-tweed arms.

Pete pulled out his phone. No texts. He checked his email. Something from Fresh Chef:

Dear Chef Pete,

We are so sorry, but our carrier has informed us that they were unable to deliver your order of the freshest ingredients this week. We specifically requested prioritized service to ensure timely delivery, but our efforts were not enough to avoid this unfortunate situation.

You shouldn't be deprived of healthy(-ish!), farm-to-fork meals, and this is certainly not the Fresh Chef experience we want for our cuisiners and cuisinières. Although it cannot make up for this disappointment, we've refunded you for this week's delivery.

We made every possible effort to re-route your delivery, but it may still arrive. If this happens, we strongly discourage you from using the contents, as the ingredients may not be up to our, or your, Fresh Chef standards of freshness.

Our deepest regrets,

The Fresh Chef Customer Experience Team

Pete raised an eyebrow. He forwarded the email to Greta, adding at the top, "THEY'RE VERY SORRY," punctuated with a screamy-cat-face emoji.

The next morning, Greta was still in bed scrolling social media when Pete arrived back from his run. The white IKEA comforter coated her like cake frosting, a sleeping Chia the cherry on top. From the sliding glass door of the balcony, sunlight moved across the milk-white walls. Greta set her phone down and looked at Pete. His red face, damp clothes, and dayglow sneakers looked incongruent in the airy room.

"Sweat monster," she said.

Pete hesitated, then thrust his knobby fists in the air. "Sweat monster hungry!" he roared, scissoring on stiff legs toward her as Chia darted out of the room. He jumped on the bed and hovered over Greta on four limbs. "Sweat monster need eat. Sweat monster eat yooooooouuuuuuuuuu," he growled as he pinned her arms.

"Stop it!" Greta screeched, writhing under him as he made biting gestures toward her head. "I'm serious!" She laughed, freeing an arm and blocking her face with an elbow. "You're dripping!"

Pete relaxed his grip. He was enjoying the last traces of his runner's high. With softened eyes, he lowered his face toward Greta's.

She scanned his downturned mouth, so close to her. "Let's wait till tonight," she said. "I'm signed up for that coffee-and-paint class this morning." She rolled out from under him. "I don't want to be late. I'm excited to do something creative."

"Okay, okay," he said, plopping onto his back. "I want to get some work done on the dissertation before your sister and Zach get here anyway." He put on a look of mock severity. "But I'm holding you to tonight, pretty lady."

"Yes, you do that." She smiled. She turned toward him, her eyes suddenly serious and empathetic. "How's the dissertation coming?"

"Coming along!" Pete lied. He had been stuck for weeks trying to show that recent advances in machine learning undermine Heidegger's phenomenological notion of dasein. The problem was that he understood neither—or at least that's how he felt on most days.

Greta studied him, slightly relieved that he didn't want to vent about his dissertation, but also wanting to be supportive. Ignoring her concerned look, Pete pulled on a strand of hair that had fallen out of her bun. "Okay," she said, stroking his arm before propping herself up to get out of bed. "I better get ready. Good luck writing." She kissed the top of his salty, wet head.

A few hours later, Greta arrived back from her coffee-and-paint class, a thin canvas boasting a golden sunflower in tow. The sunflower stretched toward the corner of the canvas across a magenta sky. She wanted to post a photo of it, but she didn't want people to think she was showing off. Maybe she would caption it, "Next time I'll try the wine-and-paint class." Still musing, she spotted the familiar red and brown cardboard box sitting on the porch. "Hey, Pete, the Fresh Chef box came," she hollered up the stairs as she entered.

"Oh yeah?" Pete called down. "Right on. They already refunded us for it." He shut his laptop and shoved Chia off his lap. He hadn't written anything anyway. He padded downstairs through the front door and inspected the box. It looked pretty beat-up. I bet we could still use most of the ingredients though, he thought.

"Maybe we can toss out the meat and still use the other stuff," he called out to Greta through the front door.

"Yeah, for sure," she called back absently as she auditioned the sunflower painting to a wall in the living room, arm outstretched, head tilted.

Pete went to lift the box. Why is it so heavy? With some effort, he lifted the box inside and dropped it on the kitchen island's countertop. He tried slicing through the box's tape with his keys, but the tape was too thick. He reached for a knife instead. Before he could pierce the top, the box jutted an inch to the left. What the hell? The box jutted again. Pete took a step back. "Um, Greta? The box is moving," he called toward the living room.

"I can't hear you. What's moving?" she called back.

"The Fresh Chef box. It like, jumped."

Greta propped the sunflower painting against the sofa and hurried into to the kitchen, Chia trotting closely behind. "What do you mean the box jumped?"

"It's moving. Watch."

They stared at the box. It sat motionless on the counter.

"Stop messing with me," Greta said, not wanting to appear gullible, her eyes fixed on the box.

The box wrenched right. Pete's and Greta's heads snapped toward each other, their eyes as alert as Chia's. They looked back toward the box, spellbound as it jerked this way and that way.

Pete sucked down a deep breath and approached the box. He planted his hand on top of it and pushed down. With his other hand still gripping the knife, he began slicing through the tape in the upper right corner.

"Wait!" Greta cried. "Maybe we shouldn't open it. I don't think we should open it."

The box lurched left under Pete's hand. He pushed down harder.

"Maybe there's a serial killer in there?" Greta said improbably. She often resorted to the improbable when reality overwhelmed.

"It's not big enough to fit a person," he replied. Of course, he knew she knew that, but Pete's statement of the obvious still emboldened him. He dragged the knife's edge through the remaining tape on the right side, then started on the left. The box doubled-down on its movements. "Here, come help me hold it," Pete said.

Greta held back for a moment, then placed her hands on either side of the box. The action reminded her of the time when she and Pete had first moved in and assembled Pete's bookcase. She had vaguely resented his prioritizing of the bookcase over the arrangement of plants and furniture on the balcony, the pièce de résistance of their modest townhouse. But as they organized Pete's books, they had delighted in inventing increasingly bizarre personal histories for the great authors and her resentment had retreated, cool beneath her waking world.

Pete tore through the final scrap of tape and met Greta's bright eyes. He grinned nervously as he lifted the top. The couple peered down. Inside the box stood a small, black pig. Its hind legs kicked as it gazed up at them, twitching two elfin ears. Its shiny jet eyes resembled those of a squirrel.

"A pig!" Greta said as she spun in a circle, an involuntary reaction to spontaneous pleasure she had had since childhood.

"A pig!" Pete said, amazed. "Why is there a pig?" He cupped his hands over his temples, elbows jutting out from his ears. They gleamed at each other like children. "This has to be a joke," Pete said as Greta twirled her body. He remembered the summer he and his big brother, Ben, had waged a practical-joke war, the long days ending with the boys clutching their bellies in fits of utterly uncontrollable laughter, the immaculate laughter of tween boys. "Maybe Ben sent it." Pete grinned. "You know what, I bet Ben sent it," Pete reaffirmed as he waved one finger in the air like a cartoon scientist. Affection for his older brother sparkled through him. Ben's commitment to a joke was something to respect.

Chia positioned herself on the floor near Pete's feet. After some peculiarly feline deliberation, she leapt onto the tile counter and sniffed the box, rapt in its unfamiliarity. From inside, the pig let out a raspy, high-pitched squeal, much louder than one would expect from a creature its size. The cat bolted out of the kitchen.

Greta orbited the box. Excitement and ammonia emanated from it. She watched the pig kick its twig-like legs under its thick, black trunk. Its tiny cloven hooves reminded Greta of an overweight woman's high heels.

Beneath the pig's hooves, shredded plastic blanketed the box's floor, presumably the remains of the farm-fresh vegetables with which it had been shipped. From under the plastic peaked the red corner of a sheet of cardstock. "Wait, Pete. There's a paper in here," Greta said. She reached in the box, careful to avoid the pig in case it bit, and pulled out a card bearing the red and white Fresh Chef logo. The pig squealed.

Pete positioned himself behind Greta to read over her shoulder, an arrangement to which she would have normally objected. She held out the card in front of them. "It's a recipe," she said. They read:

① *Prepare the Ingredients:*

☐ Using all four burners, heat four large pots of water to boiling on high.

☐ Tie the hind legs of the pig. With a large, recently sharpened knife, make a 4- to 6-inch deep incision at the throat near one ear. Cut the throat lengthwise to the other ear, making certain that the carotid and jugular are completely severed. (Tip to the chef: you may want to do this step outside.)

☐ Thoroughly bleed the pig. (See our website for a step-by-step instruction video.)

☐ In a trough (a bathtub will work if you don't have one), shower the carcass with the boiling water to remove the hair. Remove the remaining hair with a knife or razor. Re-shower the carcass with the remainder of the boiling water.

Greta had read enough. She set the instructions on the counter and covered her mouth with one hand. Pete grabbed the instructions and continued to read. They were too official to be his brother's handiwork.

Maybe I should contact customer service, Greta thought as she studied the pig in the worn box. Its tail stood on end as it met her gaze with its rodent-like eyes, ears twitching. Probably no one's working anyway, she reasoned.

Pete, remote and unguarded, continued to study the instructions. At length, he set down the recipe card and approached the box. He looked with purpose at the small, black animal ramming the box's interior with its rubbery snout. Although unmistakably a pig, there was something pug-like about it, particularly around the neck.

Pete looked up. "I think we should do it," he said.

"Oh my god, Pete. No." Greta took a step back. "We can't kill it!"

"No, we should. We eat meat, right? If we're going to eat an animal, we should be able to kill it."

"That doesn't even make sense." Greta's eyelids tore back. "We should either eat meat or we shouldn't. Whether we can kill it or not shouldn't factor in." She straightened her spine and walked on her toes closer to the box. It smelled like cat litter. "And look at him! He's so cute. And he's scared." Her throat ached. "We can't kill it." She raised her chin as if settling a point. "Besides, we rent. We can't kill an animal here. We don't even have our own yard. What, are we going to slaughter it on the balcony?" She hoped to appeal to Pete's practical side.

Pete was unpersuaded. "I mean it, Greta. I think this is something I have to do. This really resonates with me." He squared his shoulders the way his dad did when debating home-improvement projects with his mom. "I want to live in alignment. There's like this giant disconnect between how we live and where all this"—he made a sweeping gesture—"comes from. Like there's this buffer between me, us, everyone, and reality, which is fine, but it doesn't feel right. It doesn't feel good." He shuddered.

"Pete, we can't kill it. He's in our care now. You're always conflating what feels good with what's right."

"No, I'm not," he scoffed. "Listen to yourself! It's not going to feel good to kill the pig, but it's the right thing to do."

"Don't act like you don't understand what I'm saying," she said.

"I understand you. But I see this as a test—a moral test."

Greta shook her head. "Yeah, well, you're failing." She peered at the pig. Its charcoal skin shone under its wiry black coat and its tail looked like a deflated black balloon animal.

"Look, I know he's cute," Pete interjected. "But aren't all the other pigs we've eaten cute? Why should it matter that he's here?" He tensed his jaw. "If anything, that's more reason to do it. We can use all of it. Treat it as sacred. Not like merchandise. Not like a machine."

Greta could listen to no more. She stomped out of the kitchen and into the living room where she curled herself in a ball on the sofa. Her cheeks burned. Chia hopped up beside her, rubbing a whiskered cheek across her forearm. If only that Fresh Chef box had never come, she thought. From force of habit she pulled out her phone and checked social media. When she realized what she was doing she rolled her eyes and slammed the phone, oily-face down, on the sofa's arm. Chia stretched and exited the room.

In the kitchen, Pete filled their four largest pots with water, placed them on the stove, and cranked the burners to high. He examined the magnetic knife strip, its knives lined up like soldiers. He tossed open the kitchen drawers, searching for the honing steel. The key is to stay focused, he thought. Not get emotionally involved. Don't anthropomorphize it. He did his best to ignore the pig's presence, which he could feel collapsing in on him, a life moving forward.

Pete left the kitchen and went upstairs to examine the bathroom. *Maybe I can cover the floor with garbage bags.* An old jingle for a popular brand of garbage bags hijacked his mind. He shook his head to rattle it out. He lingered in the bathroom, taking refuge in the solitude and the preliminaries. He inspected the shower curtain with its school of water-stained tropical fish suspended in perpetuity on the slick plastic. *Greta never liked this curtain anyway.* He tore the curtain from the rod and spread it across the tile floor, tucking it around the toilet. The movement fortified him; he felt renewed resolve. *By doing this, I am honoring the pig. Death is the reality of my lifestyle. All lifestyles. This is the truer way to be.* He grabbed his laptop from the bedroom and brought it back to the bathroom to watch Fresh Chef's video on how to bleed a pig.

In the kitchen, Chia watched steadily, paws together, as the dented box inched closer to the counter's edge. She licked her lips. The box jerked forward until gravity took hold and toppled the box onto the floor. Out sprinted the tiny black pig. Its dainty hooves sprung and slid against the tile floor, centrifugal force pulling one side of its sausage-like torso toward the center of the earth. Chia puffed her orange fur and hissed.

The pig continued like a bullet on its trajectory, every muscle of its miniature body tight under its ebony coat. It galloped impossibly fast toward the living room, letting out a series of quick guttural barks along the way. As it rounded the corner it overturned a houseplant, spilling its deep-scented soil onto the rented carpet.

Greta jumped up and stood on top of the clean-lined sofa. She hugged her ribs and shifted her weight back and forth between her feet. The pig's boney hind legs and disproportionately large head teeter-tottered wildly as it made figure-eights around the living room. It knocked over Greta's sunflower painting, and then the guitar that Pete never played.

Greta had to do something. She made a quick break for the sliding glass door that led to a common area shared with the neighboring townhouses. She unlocked the door and slid it open. "Go out there, little pig!" she coaxed. The pig seemed to understand. It ran with abandon out the door, the vertical blinds swaying jollily in its wake. Greta watched the pig sprint across the green common lawn, the sunlight upon it, everything bright. "Du, du, du, du, du," she sang in time with the pig's rapid gait as she watched it run away.

Upstairs, Pete resisted the urge to shut off the pig-bleeding instructional video. He tried to imagine what background music would suit such a video. Certainly not the acoustic-guitar samba Fresh Chef had chosen. The video's forced neutrality only heightened his sense of unease as he watched the well-meaning hog farmer puncture the organs of a monstrously large, rust-brown pig, blood gushing by the gallon onto the earth. This is good for me, Pete told himself. I need to face this fear.

Pete's self-pep talk was interrupted by a deafening ring coming from downstairs. The smoke detector. The steam from all the boiling water must have set it off. He ran down to the kitchen, two stairs at a time. Balancing on a chair, he freed the smoke detector of its batteries. Once silent, Pete noticed the overturned box. "Oh crap! The pig got out," he hollered. Greta stood, arms akimbo, in the kitchen doorway. He looked at her. "The pig got out," he repeated.

"I know," she said. "He was running around the living room, and I let him outside."

"You let him outside?" Typical Greta solution, he thought. "We can't just leave him out there. It's a pig for Christ's sake." For Christ's sake. He never said that. Through his mind flitted an image of a middle-aged man in a red polo shirt standing tense and without joy behind a barbeque, the lawn under his feet earth-golden and dead. He sighed.

"I didn't know what to do," Greta said. "You were going to kill him."

"We have to go find it," Pete said, feeling suddenly lighter. Greta acquiesced.

Without pausing to put on their coats, the couple exited the living room's sliding glass door into the brisk fall air. They hurried to the center of the common yard and surveyed the area. No pig.

"Maybe that creeper next door stole him," Greta said.

Pete ignored her. "Maybe it ran under a bush," he said, eyeing the lawn's well-manicured perimeter. They each took a side of the yard, probing every plant they passed. Still no pig. With each vacant underbrush they came across, it seemed ever more unlikely that they would locate the pig. An unspoken relief washed over them: the problem of the pig was out of their hands.

"I think we should give up," Greta said as she neared Pete on the lawn. Before Pete could answer a shrill squeal pierced their ears. It was coming from the common area's pool.

Greta ran to the pool, Pete following close at her heals. From behind the iron gate, they saw the little black pig rummaging through the contents of an overturned garbage bin. Tail wagging, the pig bit down on a fast-food wrapper and shook it toward the sky. It dropped the wrapper and nudged its snout around the spot where the wrapper had landed.

Pete unlatched the gate, making as little sound as possible, and attempted to sneak up on the pig. The pig looked up from its garbage pile, squealed, and took off sprinting. Its hooves twinkled like a ballet dancer's pointe-shoes across the speckled pavement. Pete sprinted after it. He chased the small pig around the pool as fast as he could, but he couldn't catch it. "Come help me," he shouted at Greta, who was jumping up and down cheering them on.

With an imitation karate move, Greta positioned herself in the pig's path. She tried to grab it as it ran past, but the pig was too quick. She and Pete ran around the pool in opposite directions lunging at the pig each time it jolted past them. On perhaps the pig's 25th lap, it altered course and leapt into the pool, white water spouting like a broken fountain into the air around it. Pete jumped in after it, feet first.

The water was so cold all other thoughts vanished. As he came up for air, Pete remembered the pig. He looked around. The pig was paddling in the deep end, its black head craning out of the water. Evidently pigs can swim. He filled his lungs and crawled toward the pig. He was so cold all he could think was that he needed to get the pig and get out of the pool. He corralled the pig into the corner, where, in a hail-Mary move, he clasped the pig's compact torso with both hands. The pig thrashed and squealed. Pete brought the pig toward his chest and squeezed it hard under his arm. He climbed out of the pool still gripping the pig. "Let's get back inside," he said to Greta. She nodded.

They power-walked back to the townhouse. Under his arm, Pete could feel the wrenching animal's heart pounding. He stopped himself from sharing this fact with Greta. Inside, she took the pig from Pete and wrapped it in a bath towel. She sat on the sofa, holding the wet pig like a baby, cooing at it, while Pete went upstairs. Don't get attached,

Pete told himself as he peeled off his drenched clothes and put on a fresh pair of boxer shorts.

The doorbell rang. Maybe it's a neighbor, angry about the pig in the pool, Pete pondered. He ran downstairs and answered the door. It was Greta's sister, Nicole, and her husband, Zach. With the afternoon's porcine distractions, he had forgotten they were coming.

As they entered, Nicole maintained eye contact with Pete, pretending not to notice that he was half naked. Zach slapped Pete between the shoulder blades. "You been working out, man?" he asked. "I'd be happy to give you some pointers."

"Yeah, sounds good!" Pete said, confident he would never follow up on Zach's offer. Because who wouldn't want a software developer as a fitness guru? he felt like quipping.

Greta held the pig tightly in the living room. "Do you want to hold him?" she asked her sister.

Nicole backed away. "Ew. No. What if he has rabies?" She had never been much for animals. "Plus, there's something off about him."

Greta patted the pig's head. *Don't listen to her. There's nothing off about you*, she mentally soothed the pig.

The group formed a circle around Greta and the pig. Pete presented his case for what to do with the pig. "I think this will give us clarity," he said, wrapping up his argument. "It'll teach us what it means to be genuinely authentic, you know I mean?"

Zach, who had spent a summer volunteering on an organic farm in Bolivia, readily agreed. "You're gonna need two sets of hands, brother," he said, as he tore off his shirt.

Against Greta's heartfelt pleas and Nicole's protestations of grossness, the young men gathered their tools. They wrenched the pig from Greta and carried it upstairs and into the bathroom. Pete clutched the pig against his bare chest and Zach hog-tied its legs with twine. Zach sharpened a knife and placed it on the sink. With his tanned hands, he took the screaming pig from Pete and tried to calm it down by talking to it like it was a domesticated dog. He motioned with his head toward the knife. "You should do the honors, my friend," he said to Pete. "A rite of passage."

Pete picked up the knife. "So, you've done this before?" he asked over the pig's screeching-tire squeals.

"I haven't done it personally, but at the farm we only ate what came from the land. Usually mi hombre Arturo did the actual slaughtering though." Zach seemed unaffected by this confession.

Pete had never disliked Zach so much as he did at that moment. He took a deep breath and approached the pig. His heart thumped. It was difficult to think over the pig's screams. You don't need to think, he scolded himself. You need to act. You have to have courage.

The shower curtain stuck to Pete's bare feet. He felt claustrophobic. He swallowed and stepped closer to Zach and the hog-tied pig. The pig thrashed violently in Zach's bare arms. Pete brought the knife's edge to the pig's thick, black throat, near its elfin ear. He pushed the point of the knife in, but apparently not forcefully enough; it didn't so much as puncture the skin. The pig squealed and writhed in horror. The physical fact of the knife against the pig's throat buckled in on Pete. He felt dizzy.

He stepped back, nauseated. He paced around the cramped, wretched bathroom. Zach struggled to keep hold of the animal. Pete looked at the pig's terrified black eyes, which, behind their almond-shaped sockets, appeared rounder and deeper than his own. For an instant, the pig met Pete's eyes. Its skin rippled faintly over its muscles. Pete burned with shame.

"What's up, man?" Zach asked, feigning cluelessness.

Pete set the knife on the sink. "I can't do it," he said at length. A generous, warm nothingness swept over the crowded bathroom. "We can't kill it," he repeated. Zach pulled a face, but he did not protest.

Pete untied the pig's legs, and Zach placed it on the floor with a quick slap to its rump. The pig shrieked and ran out of the bathroom and under the bed. Pete and Zach went downstairs and informed the girls that they had decided not to go through with it. "You should've seen homeboy's face," Zach said. It was unclear whether he was talking about Pete or the pig.

That night, Pete and Greta cuddled on the sofa as the petite black pig rummaged with energy around the living room floor. Pete took videos of it with his phone. The yellow light of the corner torchier illuminated the room with a comforting and familiar glow. They repeated to each other the story, now dazzling, of how the pig had arrived in the Fresh Chef box, twirling the memory like a jewel.

From the top of Pete's bookcase, Chia stared down at the scene, eyes narrowed, ears pulled back. "Look, Chia's jealous," Greta whispered to Pete. He looked at the pissy-faced kitty, then back at Greta. They beamed at each other and laughed.

A Bus Poem:
Something Unrelated
About Mutual Suffering

Cameron Moore

You, in your white t-shirt,
your elegant smile,
and your deep dimples,
and your brown eyes—
rimmed with the fractured gleam
of drunken sunsets
brimming at the lids with nuclear tears
and misty-shined marble galaxies.
My summer paradise is really made of all these things.

Your tan skin,
stargazing between the freckles on your neck,
tracing my horoscope
across quivering constellations:
Bright red, sky-scraping angels,
wet kisses and watermelon baths.

My summer paradise is you running
after me beneath bare feet,
with a heartbeat that tastes like mango,
smells like sulfur,
stitched between seams of a velvet sky.

You don't give me butterflies—
but the fire you light
tucked tight in my rib cage
tends to attract moths.
I'd like to say I'm smarter than the insects,
but it turns out neither of us can tell
when we're too close to getting burned.

Your playful hands and the glam rock
in your car, driving all over the city.
You reach out with minty fingertips
and weave sheet music into freeway breeze
turning yellow,
ethereal,
thunderstorm hues into something so tangible
you'll miss it from the backseat.
And you are my summer paradise.

Pink sunglasses and diamond rings,
we re-new our I love yous and
forsake moonlight—
kiss me with sunshine on your lips
and scald me into bubbling stems of hydrangea.
I promise I will bloom into your summer paradise.
You love me in a sweatshirt
when my eyes are full of soft rain.
Let's buy each other chocolate,
slow dance in sweatpants,
take long walks on the beach, but vertically
so that we wind up wading too deep and
swirl into seafoam:
really, really sexy seafoam.

My summer paradise is writing you love letters.
Your small prayers,
the ones you say
when my head is on your chest.
I thank God for putting all the paradises and all the summers into you.

GETTING OUR FLICKERS
Nick Swartz

I consumed and exhausted a healthy sum of pastimes when I was in college in Michigan. I didn't work much, and my degree only required me to write bad poetry in between electives such as Wall-Climbing Techniques and Intro to Karate. Instead of trying to get dates or earn money, I simply tried to find ways to occupy myself until the point in the evening at which it became socially acceptable to drink. On one such prolonged, listless, and very dateless streak, I took to memorizing the state birds of the U.S. I had no prior interest in birds, but I had an acute interest in memorization. Perhaps I was inspired by the birds I would sometimes hear chirping through the wee hours, as if to tell me to go to bed and repeat my quotidian search for hobbies to chew up and spit out. For a short time, I tried diligently to work cactus wrens and northern cardinals into conversations with my friends and was met with a disinterest that bordered on hostility. Thus ended my fleeting days of ornithology.

That is until ten years later, after I moved to Wyoming and met and married a Westerner: Diana. We decided to join the Laramie Audubon Society and try our hands at something I had only hitherto done by mistake: birdwatching. It was Diana's idea, and it piqued my interest because of my previous brief obsession with state birds. When I relayed the story of my momentary expertise, she was mildly impressed, but once I described the dismayingly homogenous selection of state birds, my memorization feat was decidedly less meritable.

My home state of Michigan's bird is the robin, or the red-breasted robin if you feel like sounding slightly smarter. It is easy to spot because it is a boring robin. Michigan shares its state bird with Connecticut and

Wisconsin. My adopted home state of Wyoming's bird is the western meadowlark, a yellow and black bird that can be seen perched on fences screaming its song in early spring. The meadowlark, which has a great name and even better call, is tarnished by its polygamy, simultaneously wed to Wyoming, Oregon, North Dakota, Nebraska, and Montana. The mockingbird is similarly infelicitous and represents Arkansas, Florida, Mississippi, Texas, and Tennessee. Finally, the cardinal, in addition to being everyone's least favorite baseball team, is in a downright whorish relationship with six states: Illinois, Indiana, Kentucky, Virginia, Ohio, and North Carolina. Between these four indecorous species, there are only 31 states left! I briefly lived in Minnesota and was comforted by its unique state bird, the common loon, and I applauded the boldness of whoever named it, "common" and "loon" being stark antonyms. I also admire New Mexico's roadrunner for its goofy tendencies and cartoon name recognition. I spotted one once, in the hills outside San Diego, though I dared not approach for fear of being lured off a cliff or meeting my end by means of trebuchet or box of TNT. Living in Laramie convinced me that Wyoming's bird ought to be a bird of prey. I would prefer the turkey vulture to the western meadowlark, as it better represents the state's austerity and lack of water. And because springtime in southern Wyoming is little more than a Hobbesian prank—nasty, brutish, short, and 20-below with the wind chill—the most assured sign of winter's end is not the meadowlark's call, but the return of the turkey vultures to the power lines and highways where they feast on unfortunate pocket gophers.

Diana's and my descent into birding was slow and inevitable. Our graduate school courtship involved frequenting Laramie's dives—the Buckhorn, the Crow Bar, the Cowboy on 2nd (but never the Cowboy on 3rd), and Bud's. When we finished school and our friends moved to bigger cities, we abandoned the draft houses, and our lives took on a geriatric pace and simplicity. I began cooking serious adult food, things like pie crust, risotto, curry, and gnocchi. We paid attention to events like meteor showers, garage sales, and city council meetings. We found a "deer spot." I began to see sunrises that weren't the final chapter of a long night. I even built us a birdhouse when we were engaged. The next natural step was to gaze at this birdfeeder and develop some kind of connection with its diners, at least the minority who weren't squirrels. So, we took to watching birds out of our living room window, where two doves often rooted around our yard for insects and seeds that fell off the feeder, knocked down by the squirrels or the 20 or so sparrows and chickadees who came in sudden, frantic waves. I bought Diana a pair of binoculars and a field guide, and from the comfort of our den we watched, flipping through pages to try to identify these small, spastic creatures, never quite sure the difference between each species of little brown sparrows. Now and again a western tanager showed up, or a yellow warbler, something easy to ID.

Now burgeoning ornithologists, it came time to take our skills public and meet like-minded practitioners of our very Zen and mature way of life. So, we joined the Laramie Audubon Society and decided to become attendees of their bi-weekly birding events. We assumed we would be the youngest members, and the old-timers would hail us with praise for achieving bird enlightenment at such an early stage. We would not only have friends, we'd have birder friends, who would surely host potlucks and discuss interesting topics with us over quinoa salad and smoked sockeye.

When we met the group before our first Saturday morning trip, "Laramie hot spots," I was struck by the number of young men in the room, which was a local café, aptly named Night Heron. These weren't middle-aged men who'd serve us venison stew at winter poker games or old blue-haired ladies who'd come over to our house for Boggle and wine. These were twenty-somethings, like us, and even younger. They looked like Eagle Scouts who'd aged out but missed going to meetings. What on earth were all these young guys doing here? True, I was a young guy, but I was almost married and made pie crust in my spare time. These were young guys on their own. It was confusing and a little unsettling. As is customary in Wyoming, everyone was frosty toward us newcomers. We were instructed by the group leader, a young man, to meet at the greenbelt, a stretch of paved walking path that runs alongside the Laramie River and also a prime spot, we were told, for warblers.

"Wasn't the crowd I expected," Diana said as we drove to the river. It then occurred to us: these weren't man-boy scouts or members of AA trying to distract themselves away from booze. Much worse, these were graduate students. Grad students are similar to regular college students, except they are bestowed with things called "assistantships" or "fellowships," which allow them to walk a little taller with their noses slightly more slanted toward the stratosphere. These are the nauseating people who treat the word *data* as a plural—"these data are alarming."

So, there we were, a little dismayed and nervous to find ourselves among the assorted masters of science. The situation was made worse by the stark reality that I was, very recently, a graduate student myself, guilty of the same self-important offenses to which I was now witness. Realizing I was being judgmental, I swallowed my opinions and tried to remain optimistic. We had lost all of our friends, many of whom decided to continue down the academic path and pursue PhD studies, and we wanted to replace them with intelligent peers, which these people surely were. Diana, a therapist, tells me I am projecting my shame, for I had recently written a thesis that I had littered with five-dollar words and five-cent research: a "lightweight" project to be sure, something about how Detroit's 0-16 Lions team served as a good metaphor for the city itself. It's true, I was in recovery, a recent member of MA—Master's Anonymous. We resolved to be upbeat and friendly; we were there to make friends, not judgments, after all. I resolved, however, to draw the line at referring to data as anything other than a singular, mass noun, should it have come up in conversation.

We imagined birding to be a leisurely activity—a stroll down the fairway for liberal Democrats. I had purchased a large coffee at the café before the birding was to commence and soon realized that I was alone in thinking a hot, portable drink would be a good birding accessory. We began our walk along the greenbelt, and several things became evident: First, birding required two or possibly three hands—two for your high-powered binoculars or spotting scope, and one for your smartphone app to log your ID'ed species. Second, I looked like a buffoon with my 20-ounce coffee. Third, this was no stroll. It was more akin to the opening of a Best Buy on Black Friday—the birding bros power walking in chaotic zig-zags, stopping abruptly at every large bush to make bizarre swishing noises, I guess to make it apparent to the warblers that the birder group was congenial, and make it apparent to any human passersby that the birder group was completely out to lunch. Equipped with a legal pad, bulky field guide, and cumbersome drink, Diana and I tried our best to keep up, our goal simply being to learn a few new species and add them to our small, backyard birding ken. However, within the first 50 yards of our frenetic expedition, it was obvious that our most interesting observations would pertain to the behavior of the birders rather than the birds. Dozens of birds had already been spotted, identified, logged, and forgotten about before my stupid coffee cooled enough to become potable. It was the opposite of relaxing. It was like being a contestant on a long-running game show that we'd never seen and hadn't been told the rules to. Diana and I had now heard countless names of witnessed species, and I had seen exactly three birds—crows who'd scattered from the greenbelt parking lot as we'd pulled in.

Then, a promising sign: a more unified, larger commotion, with everyone looking straight ahead rather than into some far-off thicket. I could not see anything yet, but prepared mentally for a big sighting, possibly a bald eagle, possibly two, possibly fighting each other. But, alas, it was announced that it was merely something called a junco—the variety of which was now a hot debate.

"Junco? The baggy jeans from middle school?" I whispered to Diana as we adjusted our respective focus knobs. She elbowed me in the ribs, her typical response to all my jokes made in a public setting.

Meanwhile, the strange game show's two head contestants—both male grad students, one with an unkempt beard and flannel shirt (a popular look in Laramie shared by others, such as, sadly, me), the other with long blond hair and a Baby Bjorn-looking harness for his professional binoculars—argued over the sub-specie.

"Yeah, look at the distinctive dark gray hood. I'd say it's an Oregon Junco."

"Right, but the blackish lores suggest a pink-sided junco."

"I'm pretty sure—"

"I'm pretty damn sure it's a pink-sided."

"Whatever," conceded unkempt beard guy, and the group moved on, leaving Diana and me, who'd both just managed to focus our lenses on the bird.

"Based on the wingedness, colorosity, and beakiation, I'd say that's a little brown damn bird," I said and received a harder elbow.

Farther along the path, there was another moment of excitement. In plain view, actually standing in the middle of the walkway, such that even I could see and recognize it, was a northern flicker, a beautiful and sizable bird, with spots across its body reminiscent of a rainbow trout and an underwing of bright red, reminiscent of a cutthroat trout. Essentially, it was a bird that reminded me that I'd rather be fishing than birdwatching. Except I wasn't really even birdwatching; I was watching people watch birds while I spilled hot coffee down my sleeve and fumbled with out-of-focus binoculars. But this flicker presented me with my first chance to make a successful ID. With the rest of the group busy whispering their sweet avian nothings to the shrubbery, none among them had spotted what I assumed would be the sighting of the morning.

"Northern flicker!" I proclaimed. A few heads turned as the flicker fluttered away. No one unholstered their binoculars, and those who did expend a brief glance seemed genuinely annoyed that they'd wasted a second and a half on such a trivial species. Flickers, I gathered, were no prize, nor were hawks, crows, turkey vultures, or woodpeckers. In other words, cool birds were not important. This crowd favored tiny ones: the aforementioned juncos, also warblers, finches, chickadees, and sparrows, all of which have a million varieties, which allowed the birders to flex their ornithological might by offering declarations of sub-species names and Latin strings of nonsense into the ether.

The greenbelt veered from the river and, for a few blocks, cut through Laramie's west side. No longer shrouded in riparian seclusion, we emerged into a working-class residential area, sauntering slowly—like the world's most nonthreatening street gang. Suddenly, another commotion: a voice from behind from a woman in her sixties arriving late for the walk. She greeted the birder bros, who begrudgingly nodded, again perturbed by the momentary non-warbler-related happening. Then she greeted me and Diana.

"Hi, guys, I'm Darlene. Is this your first time?" she asked, noticing my coffee, Diana's field guide, and our general sense of hopelessness. "Don't worry, my sister and I have been birders for years. We just do it to relax. We don't go crazy, you know . . ." She motioned her baseball capped head toward the frantic young men, who were at that moment in another impassioned debate about some kind of water fowl called a Sabine.

"Shawn," one said, "did you get your Sabines at Lake Hattie?"

"Thursday, man. You get your Sabines yet?"

"Hell yeah, dude, got mine Tuesday night at North Crow Reservoir. Brett hasn't gotten his Sabines yet."

"Have too."

"Have not!"

And so forth, like teenagers arguing over who had reached second base with a girl. I later learned that a Sabine is a type of gull that has a completely matte-finish black head that makes them look like they reached the pond on a sky-Harley, so maybe they were worth getting excited for. Darlene asked us what we'd spotted thus far on our walk. I offered hesitantly that I'd seen a northern flicker, though I now knew that there was no inherent value in "getting your flickers."

"I love flickers!" Darlene said. Suddenly Diana and I had our friend.

"We saw some crows in the parking lot and a robin in someone's yard too!" Diana added.

"Hey, that counts. You don't have to shout things out in Latin to be a birder."

We liked this lady. Birding was her thing, but a thing among many, a hobby, a pastime. She was an enthusiast. It wasn't her "passion" nor was it or would it ever be mine. But, as good graduate students know, everyone is specialized, and to have value, one must find his or her niche. Birding was these people's lives. Bring up sports and you'd get a disdainful glare, unless the Blue Jays happened to be playing the Orioles. When I lived in Minnesota briefly, I played Scrabble somewhat competitively in the Twin Cities Scrabble Club, where there was a similar niche culture in which everybody was obsessed with the game to the point of being socially inept and out of tune with anything non-Scrabble. Conversations that didn't center around bingos, hooks, end-game strategy, or triple-triples were considered superfluous—as were romantic relationships, nutrition, and shoes without Velcro. We specialize ourselves into increasingly obscurer wedges of existence, so that eventually we feel that we are experts at something, anything, and thus we forget that we are just one of 7 billion and that in a very short time, geologically speaking, we will be dust: dead Scrabble players, extinct watchers of aquatic migratory birds, kaput backcountry snowboarders, and cremated CrossFitters.

Maybe my feelings toward the crazed young birder men were a bit of sour grapes, considering my poor performance at the pastime thus far. Anyhow, we liked Darlene. She showed Diana a free phone app that rendered our field guide obsolete. You could even log your sightings with this app, which rendered our notebook useless as well. There's no app to replace my coffee, not yet anyway, but as we neared the end of our greenbelt walk, I'd sucked most all of it down. Thus, our next destination would be one in which we would be unencumbered by such useless relics as ink, paper, or beverages. It was to be Laramie's Greenhill Cemetery, where the chickens (and crows and finches) come home to roost.

I had spent a season after graduate school working at the "cem" as the crew called it. It was, surprisingly, one of my favorite jobs. I got to tell people I "dug graves," when in reality I mainly mowed the lawn and used the leaf blower. I did, however, on occasion, dig graves, and I was surprised to discover that they were indeed dug to a depth of six feet. I'd been convinced that "six feet deep" was just a colloquialism that had a nice macabre rhythm to it—six being Mr. Satan's number of choice. But damned if it isn't true, all the more startling in southern Wyoming where the wind has kidnapped the soil's loamy organic horizon and bedrock looms very shallow wherever you're standing. There is one caveat: only "full-size" burials are six feet—full-size meaning grandpa in the big pine box wearing makeup and cowboy boots. If you choose incineration, your "cremains" are buried at a shallow 24 inches (18 if the crew is in a hurry).

Working at the cem convinced me to go "full-size" when I die, for a few reasons. First, "cremains" is a lewd and disgusting-sounding made-up word. Second, and also a matter of syntax, "cremains" are buried in "ash-holes." So, should you forgo embalming and opt for St. Peter's barbecue, know that your final role on Earth shall be as the butt of a joke, when after lunch break a cemetery crew leader will assign a 19-year-old college dropout named Derek to stick your cremains in his ash hole. Also, ashes are boring. I like the idea of rotting in the earth. I've killed enough worms while fishing to feel that they're entitled to dinner on (in) me. Finally, I don't like the idea of giving my heirs the chore of spreading my ashes at some lighthouse and making them suffer through an awkward lunch afterward. I'd rather donate my corpse to the microbial world. I don't want to be strewn; I want to be strudel.

The one condition of my full-size burial, as I will specify in my will, is that the hole be hand-dug, no backhoes or machinery, nothing that the Forest Service would deem a "mechanical advantage." As reward for the manual digging, my estate will provide the shovelers (not the species of water fowl) a case of cheap beer or schnapps, depending on the season in which I die. I hand-dug two graves the summer I worked at the cemetery, both for babies (because the backhoe's bucket is too large and clumsy for baby graves). In both instances, the crew and I took turns with shovels and picks, joking, sweating, trying not to think of the poor soon-to-be tenant of the hole, but failing. On one of the burials it was also our job to place the unborn infant into the earth after the crowd of mourners was gone, so once again by hand, we lowered a case no bigger than the one that housed my steel-toed boots, then covered it with little shovelfuls of dirt. We worked gingerly in silence, as if we believed the inscription on the grave that described the child as being at rest; a lesson in fragility that no backhoe could ever teach.

But today, Diana's and my activity was focused on matters above ground. The cemetery was a place I'd gone every day for a spring and summer and never noticed birds—living, chirping ones anyway. We came across dead crows from time to time during the big melt in April, while we were leaf-blowing the grounds, clearing the late-fall straggler leaves that detached from their limbs after the first heavy snows. Once I encountered a crow's body hidden behind a large headstone, and when my leaf blower's long barrel turned the corner, the wind lifted the crow off the ground, spreading its lifeless wings in a disturbing languid flight. It was a weird display of the Almighty's design: these were large birds, but their bodies were propelled as easily as cottonwood leaves when met with wind from the two-stroke motor.

Returning to the cemetery with the birding group clearly conjured up some memories for me. If I make it sound like a gloomy job, it wasn't. It was quite the opposite. Because the Grim Reaper was, in a manner of speaking, our foreman, it made the job strangely life-affirming. We all felt closer to death because of our unique "clientele" but also decidedly more alive. It was a great arena for deep thought as well. I remember one foggy morning in late spring, I achieved some version of Nirvana while wearing a shoulder-mounted leaf blower and foam ear plugs, clearing wet decayed leaves off headstones and burial plots. The muffled womb-like hum of the motor, the vibrations, the rhythmic back and forth of the blower tube combined with the April morning wet leaf smell and the debris scattering to reveal epitaphs—

"beloved father," "sleeping with the lord"—the names, Penny, Esther, Aubrey, Emil. It was feeling the entirety of a life cycle condensed into a moment. It is hard to describe, but if you ever see a man weeping with a leaf blower, there's a reason.

Other than the dead crows, I remember seeing a woodpecker once at the cemetery. It was on a metal pole, pecking away, which I imagine is rough on a beak. The most common bird in the cem, I thought, was what Wyomingites refer to as its real state bird: the plastic Walmart bag, or "sack" as they say in Wyoming, a word I file in the same category as "cremains" and "ash-hole."

We navigated the cemetery's perimeter, and the birding group's focus shifted to pine siskins and creepers, whose names I admired. For some reason, I liked the idea of being in a graveyard surrounded by creepers. Diana and I were actually getting the hang of things by now. We were quicker with our focus nobs and better at judging the angles at which to crane our necks. I couldn't say I was enjoying birdwatching, but at least I didn't feel like a big bumbling oaf anymore. Next the group spotted some Townsend solitaires, also fantastically named birds. Then one of the grad students excitedly but quietly motioned us toward one of the cem's large lilac bushes, where a bright yellow warbler was perched. One thing about male birds is that they don't play hard to get; the brighter the better as far as they're concerned. Their plumage says, "I'm dressing this way for you." It's honest. Birds don't passively write poems and act mysterious to attract women. They put on their brightest outfits and strut.

Shawn, the leader of the group, approached the bush with his camera, making his curious swishing noises. The bird noticed him and performed a quick calculation in his head to determine whether the human was a threat. He wasn't, and the bird stayed while Shawn took his photograph. The warbler then fluttered away to a different bush, not because he appeared threatened but because we were probably preventing female birds from coming into his turf.

It was the sighting of the day and one that didn't even require anyone to fumble with binoculars. It was a good time for the walk to end. We had circled back to near the front gate of the cemetery, and now were in a row of graves I recognized, having mowed it many times.

"Good day for creepers," one of the older men said.

"Warblers were out, too," added one of the grad students.

Standing in a loose circle, the group's attention briefly shifted to me as people added their closing summations. I pointed to a headstone: Benjamin Franklin Bird. "I think this was my best sighting of the day," I said, finally earning a chuckle from the serious birders.

Diana and I hadn't found our calling, but we had done something nice with our Saturday morning. Driving home from what I had initially considered one of my great hapless follies, of which there are many, I realized that there was value in our attempt at birding. My thoughts during the remainder of the day repeatedly returned to that yellow warbler conducting his solitary and deliberate affairs. This bird encapsulated the essence of why we're attracted to watching birds and other animals. They have the ability to behave without a conscience, to strip down life into a clear set of needs and direct their entire existence to achieving concrete ends. We watch animals because we are jealous of them. Perhaps the ultimate goal in life is to forsake our human cognition while retaining enough of it to realize we are doing so. When we get to that point we become the bright yellow warbler, sitting in the bush, with no thought other than to complete his life's work. We can then peacefully join the rest of humanity in the ground underneath the cemetery lilacs.

NATURALLY

Mika Hunter

It was liberated
from what had been
abducted by some bright
white substance, she
discovered deep dark
black.

What she discovered was
complex. It was falsely
convicted for decades
because of lies that
were told.

Unpretty, nappy, dry
and brittle, Gurl,
you need to go fix
yo hair. The original
defendants became
the prosecution.

Grandmasters of lies
told. Brainwashing
those . . .

Changing the entities'
uniqueness. Tricking
the pawns to believe its
ancestral truths were
lies.

Well, the pawn just
made it to the other
side . . . where its
ancestral roots naturally
reside.

A MONSTER'S EULOGY

Rekha Rangan

I don't like children. My sister, Claire, says I just don't know what to do with them. Like a vegan with a steak. Or an atheist with one of those wallet-sized pictures of Jesus. Or, I guess, a religious person with a picture of an atheist.

Everyone knows it by now. It gets harder to hide that part of yourself. People catch on pretty quickly when you smile a half a second too late when their kid does something adorable (boring), or if you don't show enough concern when they do something stupid (hilarious). When we were all at Mary-Anne's birthday party last year at the park next to the creek downtown, Claire's youngest spawn, Joseph, biked straight into a brick wall that he'd clearly seen coming from a mile away. No one else saw it happen except me, and when I started laughing, he stared dry-eyed at me for a solid minute until Claire showed up, at which point he remembered to start crying.

"Something's wrong with you," Claire said to me while wearing a bright, conical party hat with a clown's head impaled on the tip. She has eleven years on me, and for as long as I've known her, there wasn't a time when she didn't have a baby in her arms, plastic or otherwise. Claire is also the least patient person I know. She always definitely wanted to be a mom, but only for kids she liked.

Today she says, "Your impassivity concerns me." Claire likes to open her dictionary up to a random page, pick the longest word, and throw it into conversation for the rest of the week. She's standing in the kitchen holding a knife in one hand and a glass of red wine in the other. I wonder why I'm the only one who's ever concerned by her.

"Impassivity" has five syllables, so that means five slices of pear. They come out like translucent sheets, the stripped wings of a butterfly. She flowers them out onto a plate next to a handful of broccoli and other fruits and places it at the center of the marble island. Then she glances out the kitchen window hopefully, likely imagining what it would be like if her kids would come rushing in from playing chess, straightening their frocks and ready to snack on geometrically equivalent slices of grapefruit. Right now, her eldest daughter is shoving a mound of grass in her mouth.

She wipes her hands against the kitchen towel tucked into her belt. "You can still come to Mary-Anne's recital tonight."

"No thanks," I say. If there's anything worse than a stage full of kids that know they have your undivided attention for an hour, it's when those kids have musical instruments.

Claire expresses her disapproval with a quiet *hmph*. I don't understand the stigma. People are allowed to not like dogs or cats. And that's not to say babies are pets—pets are easier—but, they have a lot of similar qualities: drool, an inability to comprehend basic language, can't clean up their own shit. I don't get how you can love something that much after you've cleaned its shit.

I eye the books stacked up on the end table beside the floral-printed couch, tucked against the bowl of potpourri in a pretend-effort to hide them: *The Sociopath Next Door: Understanding Psychopathy*.

I move over to sit by them in the conjoined living room. My feet burrow into the handwoven alpaca-fur rug that Claire doggedly insists a close friend in Peru sent her. Her close friend eBay.

"Finally planning on doing some internal reflection?" I ask.

"Don't get so defensive," she says flatly. "I'm just concerned. You know, that kind of thing is genetic. I have to be prepared. If you have it, there's a good chance one of my kids could have it, too."

"What, common sense? Self-respect?"

"I'm being serious, Em."

"Maybe you're right." I open one of the books—*The Signs of Sociopathy* by James Clark—and lay it out over my lap. "Symptoms of sociopathy. Charming? Check. Intelligent? Check. Lack of sex drive? Oh, Mr. Clark, you're making me blush."

A lawn mower starts up in a nearby backyard, only barely muffled by the glass. Claire looks like she wants to throw me under it.

"Honestly, you're so resentful. I wish you would see that therapist, I really do." Back to the pear, chop chop chop. "I think you could really make some improvements." She likes to discuss my mental health like it's a house she can renovate.

"I don't need a therapist."

Claire slides the rest of the pear onto the plate and sets her knife down hard enough to make the cutting board tremble, all in one motion. She takes a long sip of her wine, sucking lightly at her teeth before clearing her throat and bracing herself against the edge of the counter.

"Emily, I've been really patient with you. I always have. But I can't keep pretending everything's fine."

I continue to flip through the pages of the book, admiring the lack of any citations or sources. "You definitely haven't been."

"You never even apologized to her."

"I did apologize to her, even though it wasn't my fault."

"Taking her to Cold Stone isn't an apology, Emily." Claire is only just getting the ball rolling, I can tell, because the only time there's ever any sign of life in her eyes is when she's preparing a tirade. "And ice cream didn't pay the medical bills. Ice cream didn't make her less frightened to cross the street."

The backs of my hands are starting to itch where they'd dried up across the knuckles. Things that trigger eczema: Stress. Irritants. My sister.

I stand, calculating how many large strides it'll take me to get to the door. "Thanks for the pasta, Claire-Bear. I saw one of your neighbors repainting his fence, and I really want to see if I can make it over in time to watch it dry, so I should head out."

Claire trails after me to the door. She always stomps after you and lurks just far enough that you can't hit her. "Well, I hope you have another sister you can freeload off of on Thanksgiving."

"Because last year will be so hard to beat." After Joseph dumped the mashed potatoes, green beans, and most of the carved turkey into the downstairs bathtub and turned the faucet on, Claire dragged me out to WinCo to use my employee discount on whatever cheese and cracker assortments they had left. At the checkout, the woman in front of us had two items in her basket: a 12-pack of Charmin rolls and a family-sized bottle of Jack Daniels.

"That will be you one day, if you don't get it together," my sister told me under her breath.

"Hey, at least I'll still use toilet paper."

Since the day of the accident, after she took my keys and found all the bottles in the trunk of my car, that's all she sees when she looks at me. A giant bottle of whiskey. The irony of the whole thing is that I don't drink—hate the taste of it. But I have plenty of friends who do, and after every party, they'd leave their bottles scattered out across tables and carpets—the dark-tinted, the swan-necked, the ones that looked like old-timey perfumes—and I'd pick one up and take it with me. I've always collected things: oddly shaped rocks when I was 7, seashells when I was 11, broken watches from thrift stores when I was 15.

Claire collects things, too. More specifically, boxes. They're the first thing I see as I slam the door shut, piled at the end of her driveway where they fill up and spill out over her recycling bin. She orders everything online. Everything. Toothbrushes. Paperclips. She one time even ordered cardboard. She wouldn't dare touch any from the unlimited source out on her front lawn—she needed it fresh, free-range, and whole grain.

I pass the boxes and head for my car on the street. Leaving my sister's house has always given me the most cathartic feeling, and I'm aching for it now, but I have to stop when I get to the sidewalk. Crouching by the front wheel is one of my sister's kids, Tim.

It's hard to describe Tim. I can try out words on him like clothes, but none of them ever fit. Isolated and depressed are too baggy and boring and aimless is too tight. The best description I can come up with is just middle-child. He's staring into the gutter, shoelaces stuffed into the sides of his sneakers.

"What're you looking at?" I ask.

Tim curves his palms over his knees. His hands are evolutionarily adapted for that purpose. "A worm. It's dead."

Though I've seen plenty of dead worms in my life, I still lean over to get a look. Pasty and wet, it does indeed look dead.

"Cogent observation."

"Cogent?"

"Look it up. And use it in front of your mom, it'll piss her off."

"Okay," he says, drearily. "I wish this worm wasn't so dead."

"Some things are better off dead."

"I don't think so."

I can remember all of three times when I've seen Tim smile. In every other moment of his life that I have borne witness to, his eyes were pinned to things that no one else could see, things that made his eyelids droop and his face gray. There are little things I notice about him that don't fit. Like, the way kids always ask for your stuff. Your slice of cake. The seashell you found. Your necklace. But not Tim. Tim never wanted a thing.

I consider him for a long moment, then ask, "You ever been to a funeral before?"

Tim shakes his head slowly.

My sister's entire front lawn is extremely well trimmed and a kind of fluorescent green that looks Photoshopped, and digging a hole there would be even more therapeutic than just leaving. But she loves her potted ferns more, so I choose one from where they line her walkway up to the door and rip the stem out, tossing it into the neighbor's yard. I set the pot on the sidewalk in front of Tim, where he cradles the worm carcass in his hand.

"Put her in," I say. Tim blinks in the space of time longer than it took mankind to civilize, then kneels down to plant the worm in the dirt. We both stand over the pot in silence until I finally clear my throat.

"We're gathered here today in remembrance of Jane Doe, the worm."

Tim stares up at me, waiting for me to continue. I shrug. I've never been to a funeral, either.

"Jane Doe was a worm," I go on. "An unremarkable worm. But most worms are, so she really shouldn't take it personally. I guess she was just trying to fight her predetermined worth. She didn't win, but she tried really hard, and then she died. Just like the rest of us will." I nodded at Tim. "Any other words before her burial?"

"I think she should be cremated," Tim says. "I think that's what she wanted."

"You discussed this with her family?"

"I think we're her family."

"Right. Well, I have a lighter in my car, but damp soil isn't really going to burn."

"Alcohol burns," he says, like a budding arsonist.

"I don't have alcohol."

"Mom says you do."

"Your mom's an idiot. You should tell her that, too." I watch Tim for a minute, right at the scalp line that paves the way of his cleanly parted hair. "Do you believe your mom? About me?"

When Tim tilts his head in thought, it looks like he's slowly losing the ability to hold it up on his own. "She says a lot about you."

Don't ask. Not worth it.

"Like what?"

"You don't say thank you for things."

"In order for me to say thanks, she would need to do something I'm thankful for."

"She talks about when you guys were little." Tim is kneeling again, his arms tucked in against his stomach as he peers into the soil. "She says me and Mary-Anne and Joseph have to be better."

When we were little. It's not like my sister and I were ever little together. She was always a grown-up to me, being so much older. We never liked each other, but back then, it was different. We both found a common enemy in an empty house. She'd at least come home, even when no one else did.

My stomach aches and my nose burns with the tang of freshly cut grass. "How about I cremate her later? Let's put her in my car."

Tim's shoulders are at his ears trying to carry the pot, but it seems like this is something he wants to do on his own. As he takes his first step, his heel comes down on a loose shoelace, and that's it. He performs an involuntary somersault down onto the asphalt and the soil sprays out around him like blood at a crime scene. After a moment, he sits up, dirt trickling down from the creases between his eyes and nose but not bleeding out from anywhere important.

My first reaction is to laugh, but I try to choke it back as my sister trots out, ready to unload another cardboard box, but most likely checking to see if I've actually left. When she sees Tim, she screams and drops her box, her flip-flops slapping the pavement as she stumbles over to him.

"Oh god, Tim, my baby, are you all right?" She starts pulling at all his limbs, pausing when she gets to his elbow, where a red patch begins to pulse with a grid of blood.

"I'm okay," he says, but she hears, "I'm dying, Mother, and it's Emily's fault."

"What did you do?" she yells at me.

"Nothing," I say. "He tripped over his shoelace."

"If you saw them all over the place, why didn't you tell him to tie his shoes?"

"He's nine."

"Yes, he's nine. He's a child. Use your head, Emily!" She grips Tim's wrist like she's the only thing holding him together. "I swear, you do these things on purpose."

Everyone has a limit.

"Claire." I'm serious, as serious as she wanted me to be ten minutes ago. "I wish I hadn't hit Mary-Anne. I wish she hadn't broken her leg. I also wish that you didn't have so many goddamn boxes that your stupid kids can hide under, and I wish you'd been out there watching your goddamn offspring if you really care as much about them as you say you do, and I wish you'd face your screwed-up idea of parenting instead of assuming I'm an alcoholic, and I'm not out to get you. I'm not out to ruin your sad, pathetic, shitty suburban existence."

Claire hobbles up onto her feet, and she starts her words with exaggerated breaths. "Oh, for God's sake, stop lying to everyone, stop lying to yourself." She almost kicks Tim, who doesn't move, sitting there and staring blankly at his mother's toes. "Just tell the truth for once."

I have a lot of truths. I'm not a bad person. I donate blood, every eight weeks, on the dot, and I don't wear the free T-shirt around the next day. There's an orange tree in my front yard that refuses to die, and when the oranges fall off in the spring, I box them up and give them to my neighbors. I help people with their cars when they need a jump-start on the side of the highway. None of these truths are the ones my sister is looking for.

I pull my car keys out and open the front door, and my sister shakes her head. "You're a natural disaster, you know that? You just screw everything up and walk away."

"Bye, Tim," I say.

He holds up a palm.

I don't like kids, but I don't hate them. I don't like my sister, but I don't hate her.

When I see my sister with my eyes open, I see her swollen cheeks as she kneels on the driveway, rubbing potting soil into the knees of jeans she'd ironed stiff. When I see her with my eyes closed, I get other things. Older things. When she'd get off early from work at Irene's Diner and roll up to school just as I was about to get on the bus. Or when she'd walk me to the park when I was six and I didn't know how to get there on my own. Or when I was nine and I threw away the letter my teacher sent home with me, advertising my school's open house. My sister showed up at school two days later, staring at my painting of a tree. There were 22 other trees there, but she was just staring at mine.

When I blink, I see her then and I see her now, but the in-between isn't there. I don't know when she got so sad, or when she began to convince herself I was the reason for it.

As I drive, I miss the clanking of the bottles in my trunk. I like to collect things. My sister does, too. She wants ugly things. She wants lies, she wants justifications. She wants me to say it. She wants me to believe that I'm the monster she needs me to be. But monsters don't bury the dead.

An Inconvenient Death

Gabriella Buckner

At the funeral they hand out blue horses.
Someone took your painting
to the Print and Copy center of an Office Max
and for 50 cents a page
bred a watercolor army
of the last thing your hands could make.

They used to make everything,
when the summers were warm peaches
and dragonflies glittering in the heat
and your legs were cacti pricking me
with stubble.
You just laughed when I itched on your lap
and came with Grandpa every day to
pass on the knowledge of the lines
it takes to make a cat or a bunny
on sketch paper.

But the peaches oozed into a brown mush
with no one there to pick them.
After chemo I didn't sit on your lap,
not because you were too weak,
but because I was twelve
and a twelve-year-old has better things to do
than touch legs that aren't cacti anymore,
but a desert with the sand
blasted away to the cold,
sad, flesh of the earth underneath.
A twelve-year-old is trying on bras
and buying hair spray
for the first time,
and your head was an egg we were afraid to drop
because everyone knew
it would never make it to springtime.

At the service, they cry like people
often do and hold onto each other like each arm
is the last scrap of wood from the *Titanic*
but thoughts of my latest crush keep me buoyant
on the sidelines as I watch.
Then someone hands me a blue horse.
It seems majestic, galloping against a background
you didn't have time to paint.
But as the priest begins to intone words I have no ears for,
I can see the outlines in the death-white
of the blank paper:
the horse stomping into the dirt,
searching through the chunks of me
for the scent of someone
it could recognize.

Dangerous Fish Days

Robert Hambling Davis

The tide rolls in with a warm April breeze, south of the boardwalk in Rehoboth Beach, Delaware. I come here when the crowds are gone and I can embrace my solitude. My mother took me to this spot to see the sea for the first time, a year after I'd immersed myself in its depths. I sit on her patchwork quilt of hex signs, the one she brought with us on that day long ago, along with her scrapbook of my drawings. The book has twine binding and a brown leather cover. I open it to a crayon drawing of a black thresher shark baring its teeth at a giant yellow squid. The squid has its tentacles wrapped around the shark. The sea is green and streaked with red. The pink man in the submarine grins, watching the fight through the porthole. He doesn't see the humpback whale about to bite off his periscope. As I study this drawing I feel like I was born under the sea, among coral and crustaceans, and raised to swim with dangerous fish.

My mother supplied me with crayons, pencils, and sketchpads, and I spent my preschool days on the living room floor, searching the dictionary for pictures of fish. When I found one I ran out to the kitchen, flapped the book by her feet, pointed at the picture, and said, "Can it eat me, Mama? Can it eat me?"

She stopped ironing or cooking, knelt by my side, and examined the tiny black and white picture in the margin. If it was a bass or trout and she said no, I resumed my search for the man-eaters of my dreams. If it was a fish she never heard of, she read the definition out loud and sometimes held the book at arm's length, as if at this distance the fish might tell her what it wanted for dinner. Confessing she didn't know was the same as saying the fish was harmless. But when I found a shark and she said, "Yes, I think it could eat you," I ran back to the living room, drew the fish repeatedly, and tossed my pictures helter-skelter, covering the floor in a flood of horror.

How did my mother account for my strange and prodigious output? How did she decide what to save? Which drawings would delight me the most when I grew up and revisited my Neptunian boyhood? I never asked. It's a mystery to savor, not solve.

As I made my way through Webster's, I came to O and my biggest thrill, the octopus. I drew it with extra-long tentacles and Big Bad Wolf eyes. I drew it dueling narwhals, great blues, and deep-sea divers with knives longer than their legs. Though not dangerous, the slimy mollusk and its leech-like suckers and shroud of black ink gave me gooseflesh and a racing pulse.

Living on a secluded horse farm in north Delaware encouraged my shyness. When I turned 5 my mother, who'd taught elementary school for 12 years, told me I could go to kindergarten or stay at home. I chose home.

Each morning she got out her flash cards and we had school at the kitchen table. On each of the cards she'd painted in watercolor a letter of the alphabet and something whose name began with that letter. O showed an octopus, its tentacles like fried strips of liver; S a stingray, whose spiny black tail looked like a train track; and the whale on the W card was brown, its spout a sprig of green. D stood for distelfink, the totem bird my mother's people painted on their barns, along with hex signs, to ward off evil. With its red body, blue feathers, and long yellow tail, it matched the ones she'd painted on the crown molding in our kitchen.

When I closed my eyes each night in bed, I saw my mother's paintings. When I said the name of whatever I saw, I remembered the right letter and said it too. Soon I was reciting the alphabet, then falling asleep and dreaming in watercolor.

The surf streams up the beach. Gulls circle and dive. The wind rustles my scrapbook. I turn the page. A diver fights an octopus and hammerhead shark at the same time. The shark is trying to chomp through the diver's lifeline. The octopus has kinked his air hose. Starfish surround his boots on the ocean floor. Bug-eyed sea horses watch from the sidelines. Does he stand a chance with that knife?

I penciled this drawing when I was six, and my mother sent it to our town paper. When the drawing appeared on the front page, my first-grade teacher Miss Sutcliff asked me to bring it in for show-and-tell. I brought in the drawing but was too shy to talk about it. Miss Sutcliff praised my talent and passed around the newspaper copy. She hung my drawing on the bulletin board, got out cookies and milk, and invited us to an "art show." I stuffed my mouth with Oreos, prickling with heat as the other kids gawked at my drawing and then at me.

"Today is a holiday," Miss Sutcliff said.

"What is it?"

"Dangerous Fish Day."

My classmates looked puzzled.

"You've never heard of Dangerous Fish Day because we are celebrating it for the first time." She held out her arms as if hugging us. "Just think how special you are."

She called us up to see pictures of dangerous fish she'd put on the show-and-tell table and then told us to draw them. We ran back to our desks and took out our crayons and paper. The room got quiet. I dashed off drawings of saw-toothed piranhas, killer whales with bloodsucking remoras stuck to their bellies, and a gang of moray eels chasing a scuba diver.

Miss Sutcliff walked around, inspecting our work in progress. "Carl, I love your shark. It looks so dangerous. And Regina, is that an underwater dinosaur? I sure wouldn't want to tangle with it. Keep it up, all of you. You are bold swimmers diving deep. Draw! Draw! Draw with all you've got!"

She had each of us hold up a drawing and name the fish that it showed. We stood by our desks, holding our pictures over our heads and singing our deep-sea roll call. She showed us pictures of the Loch Ness Monster as it burst from the depths, gaping its jaws at fishing sloops. We oohed and ahhed and drew our own renditions.

Miss Sutcliff told us to tape our drawings to the walls wherever we wanted. "Don't forget the cloak room," she said, and a bunch of us rushed the door to the dark back room.

When we returned to our desks, she said, "Now we'll all do the Octopus Walk. It's the best thing to do on Dangerous Fish Day. The Octopus Walk must have a leader." She looked around the room, then at me, and asked if I'd be the leader.

"Yes!" I hollered, and dove onto the floor. I snaked my arms and head about, crawling in oozy spurts. My classmates and Miss Sutcliff slithered behind me. The room whirled and rocked. The sea was in our blood. What a holiday!

The next year I entered the Delaware State Science Fair with a plaster of Paris profile of a sperm whale on poster board. I drew arrows to different parts of the whale's anatomy and drew and labeled commercial products containing these parts, such as face creams and cooking fats made from blubber oil, and a perfume preservative from ambergris, an undigested waxy lump found in the intestines. I glued to my poster a sperm whale's tooth a sailor had given my mother when she and my father sailed to Aruba on their honeymoon. I won Honorable Mention for my entry, long before *Save the Whales!* became a catchphrase.

My obsession peaked when I turned eight and asked my mother to read *Moby Dick* to me. She agreed without so much as a moan or look of dread, then repeated one of her favorite expressions: "Nothing is ever easy."

The reading took place in her room. I lay on her bed, up to my chin in her tulip quilt. She sat in her armchair, under good light, and took up the unabridged edition with its dust jacket of a three-masted ship, harpooners in boats, and an oyster white whale on a steel blue sea. She launched into that complex tome, reading however much she could bear at one time. She did her best to pronounce the big words and Melville's ponderous phrases, and didn't ask me how much I understood. A little each night, each night without fail, she attacked that multi-layered tale of vengeance, that prophetic song of the sea, the bulk of which surpassed my comprehension. Her reading made me sleepy, and what it did to her I never asked, though I never saw her stifle a yawn during this prolonged bedtime ordeal.

Ishmael, Ahab, Queequeg, and the white whale swam in my brain as she read on, over that winter and spring, skipping no sections, not even those metaphysical digressions on cetology. When the *Pequod* finally sank in the leviathan's wake, dandelions had gone to seed and bullfrogs croaked by our fishpond.

Forty years later I was living in the second house on the farm, the one we used to rent out when I was a boy, across the field from my mother's house. Christmas trees had replaced the horses. She liked to take walks between the rows of spruce and pine.

"Out for my health," she said, stopping to visit with a ham hock for my elkhound. We went down to the fishpond and sat on the dock.

"Next you'll have them jumping through hula hoops," she said, as the sunnies nibbled bread crumbs from my hand. Her hair was silver white, her laugh still quick and easy.

Cars and motorcycles zoomed along the road. A shopping center, golf course, and townhouses had replaced the dairy and rabbit farms, but on this side we'd lost only one 90-foot sycamore at the end of our lane when the road was widened.

My mother had bought a new Honda she didn't drive at night. "Who'd ever think I'd pay more for a car than your dad and I paid for this farm in 1942?" She rolled her eyes and laughed. "I love my Honda. I'd better, don't you think?"

She laughed at her own jokes. Once, when I asked her why, she said, "Why miss out on half the fun?"

She believed in common sense, which for her meant living enthusiastically. Common sense was something almost everyone had, but rarely used to its fullest potential. She never questioned whether this was the best of all possible worlds. That it was the only world she knew was enough for her to spend each day enjoying it, instead of speculating on what life would be like in Heaven, Hell, or on Mars.

She walked back toward her house, past pokeweed and Queen Anne's lace. She favored her right leg as she entered the path through the pines. Geese sailed over the barn. A cool breeze rippled the pond. Autumn was in the air.

I waited on the dock until I saw her on the far side of the field. Then I tossed the last of my bread on the water. The sunnies scattered as a largemouth bass streaked up from below.

The tide has gone out in the late afternoon. Gulls and the breakers and a dog in the distance make the only sounds. I close my scrapbook and stand up. I feel my mother standing beside me as she did when she brought me here for the first time. It was a warm spring day like today. She spread her quilt on the sand while I gazed at the sea.

"All the fish you draw, they're all out there," she said, her polka dot skirt rippling in the wind. She knelt and held her hand on my chest. "And they're in here too. Even the killer whales and great white sharks. There's room for them all, from the smallest to the biggest."

"Mama," I said, "if they're all inside me, they didn't eat me. I ate them."

"Yes," she said and laughed.

Dear Demeter

Audrey Larkin

Mother,
I cannot wait to be deep in the caverns of the world.
My sun-tarnished tresses making way for a darker color.
Newly pale skin caressed by vibrant silks held in place with jewel
encrusted pins.
Gifts from my husband who missed me in my forced absence.

You, my overbearing mother and all of your watchers, with mysteries
wrapped up in secrets.
You are too young, you said, too innocent for this world.
Where would you be without us? To keep you safe? To keep you
sheltered?

You kept me blind.
I have found that one can long for things unknown,
Not realizing they were missing till the cracks had been filled.
A hand presented, a chance to run away.
I wanted to be alone. Or have a connection that wasn't superficial.
To be observed, not watched. Protected but not smothered.
Balanced by someone who is not you.

Tall, dark, and lonely.
How long can he spend alone in the dark?
How many judgments could he make without feeling judged himself?
To be constantly upright, unable to falter.
How can one bear such a burden without something to lighten the load?

Perpetually kept young.
Perpetually trimmed like a manicured garden.
Maintaining a spring-like image.
I want to be wild.
A flower that grows in the cracks of the earth, alone except for the
stone that supports it.
I want life with a little more meaning, a little deeper connection.
Strong roots against secure anchors.

I am the only bright thing in his world and he is my strength,
My gracious lover, attender to every need.
No longer a bud among flowers.
I have been transplanted.
Taken from the overcrowded, clamoring garden,
Allowed to bloom in a place with enough space to press my limits.

All those things you said I could never be.
Look at me now. What do you see?
Am I as timid as you wanted?
You spit spite at me, now that you've taken me back
To this crowded conservatory turned Coliseum.
All heads turn to witness this scene you cause.
Vixen. Whore. Dirty. How could I?
What was I thinking? To stay willingly in the darkness?

Well I ask you this.
Who are you to stay in the light?
When I have watched as your guilt processed passed my lover and me.
Do you know the pain you brought him? The sleepless nights?
The never touched plates? The "I'm not hungry, dear," dinners,
Or the "Go without me, I'll join you as soon as I can," evenings,
The nights I lie alone, waiting for him, only to wake and find him
asleep at his desk.

I swear his body wasted away before my eyes.
While he worked himself near death, you ignored your work.
Froze the world. Killed those who loved you.
You say he stole me, but you drove me to him in the first place.
And now all you want is to forget? The cold? The hunger?
Wash it away with frigid warmth, false smiles,
Biting words smoothed over by controlling touches?
I think not.

I think
That you want me to stay young, innocent, stupid.
Not because it's good for me, but because you never outgrew that stage
yourself.
Froze your time at the moment of my birth.
Took your world and wrapped it tight around me like a swaddling cloth.
Maybe you thought that would solve everything.
If you could control me, you could control your world.

But I am more than you.
You are a part of me, yes. I love you. I do.
But while you made me your everything, he became mine.
He loved me enough to let me go.
He loved me enough to tell me everything.
He gave books, and stories, and nights where tears carved relived
memories down his cheeks
And I took them, giving my own back in return.
I was not lesser with him, even though I am so much younger.
I was equal. Taught. Respected. Listened to.
I was Queen. To Him. To his people.
The only one who doesn't seem to see is you.
But then again, it's always about you, isn't it?

Your time with me is up.
I willingly run from this too sweet surface.
Back to my home, to my love, to my world.
Where the fires of Phlegethon light our skies
And Asphodel reflects the souls that move throughout my wild gardens.

Back to my window seat in his office with my table and my tea.
Half a pomegranate each. How we should be.
He does his work. I keep him calm
And when it all gets too much,
I turn off the light,
Guide him out the doors, to our room.
Where I'll hold him till the stress falls from his shoulders.
Then the next morning, he'll kiss me awake
Tell me about his dreams or the trips we will take.

That is a life.
It's not superficial or perfect, but that's all I want.
So, beg again.
Tell me why I should stay.
You offer me flowers and veiled words covered in spite.
I don't think you were listening.
You don't need to tell me I'm right.
I'm going back home to where my happiness is.
He waits for me now, the lights all lit.
He's probably pacing the shore, my perfect fit.

There is more to the story than you will remember,
But most of that you will forget.
You'll tell the world what you think happened.
It won't be right, but maybe, just maybe, someday you'll ask me to tell
the story again.
Of how we fell in love in a moment and have been that way ever since.

No longer yours,

Persephone, Queen of the Dead

DISRUPTING HISTORY

Mariya Taher

For almost a decade I've been writing about female genital cutting (FGC), the act involving partial or total removal of the female genitalia, or other injury to a woman's genital organs for nonmedical reasons.

Upon first wondering about it, my response was almost clinical: I was curious; for example, what were the mechanics of FGC? How had the practice started? Why was it performed? What actually was done to a girl? As someone with an unquenchable thirst for knowledge, I looked to the academic world to understand this act's intricacies. Facts. School trained me to find them, to be analytical, to cite sources, to have faith in scholarly work. So, I turned to academia to be my trusted friend, my advisor, my teacher.

I read case studies, qualitative studies, quantitative studies, and literature reviews. I printed reports and scrutinized the black letters on the multitude of white pages in every report. I pulled up PDF documents accessible via JSTOR, the digital library of academic journals, books, and primary sources, and stared at my computer's screen until my eyes were met with strain. I did not need images of flesh and blood people to engage in this quest for information about female genital cutting. Research techniques I had been trained to use allowed me to contemplate the inner workings of this practice in a removed but scholarly manner. No emotion was involved. I could "other" the problem. After all, it happened to "those people" living in those other places outside the United States.

Except this is not the entire truth. I assumed academe could be my protector, yet since childhood, I'd had an intimate connection with this subject, and so I wasn't an impartial researcher. I never could be.

Female genital cutting happened to me. It was part of my history. At the age of seven, my mother took me to have it done as her mothers had taken her. The tradition went back generation after generation in my family; it was a "necessity" mothers ensured continued to their daughters so we all grew up to be pure, morally sound Dawoodi Bohra Muslim women. This act they did out of love. The day it was done to me, I wore a frilly dress that was pulled up to reveal my midriff and underwear that was pulled down to reveal parts I had been taught were to remain private.

At the time, I knew the practice as "khatna."

The truth was that I was the subject of my research. I was a type—an FGC type. There are four, I learned, as defined by the World Health Organization. What happened to me was roman numeral Type I FGC, the least severe: a pinch of skin removed from my clitoral hood. I underwent it because our community held it to be a religious obligation. It had to be done, I was told, to decrease my sexuality. The idea of a promiscuous woman was forbidden, an uncut woman would become just that—a lover of sex with multiple men, something considered haram. My mother told me this. The research I found suggested her explanation was a common one given to many girls raised in communities where FGC was practiced.

But, in my reality, my mother had me undergo it because she loved me. She was taking care of me. She always took care of me. During childhood when I coughed, when snot dripped from my nose, when I whimpered because my body ached with fever and chills, she cared for me. The devotion and love she expressed when I was sick was of the same breed that led her to take me to a dilapidated apartment building where I would undergo my khatna, and afterwards have her comfort me.

I have no doubt of this truth.

But neither my mother nor the research I found could explain to me how the act of cutting one's genitals had even become associated with the idea of love in the first place. What had given khatna the gold star status it held, and encouraged women like my mother to carry the tradition onto their daughters and for religious leaders in my community to preach its necessity, even after many countries passed legislation criminalizing the act (the United States banned it in 1996, seven years after it was performed on me)?

I needed to understand.

I did more research and found more gaps in the information. Every report I read stated the practice was primarily found in Africa, but I was born in the United States. I underwent the cutting one summer on a trip to India to visit relatives, a trip my family made every two years of my childhood. The research had not counted me. Academia had failed to include me. My trusted friend was not as reliable as I had originally believed. My story was untold. I did not count.

I needed my story to count.

I needed to become the researcher. The person who would gather the information, write the report, and disburse the information far and wide. During my stint in graduate school for my master of social work degree, I got my chance. I talked my advisors into letting me craft my own research project. I molded academia into a form that would allow me to understand FGC. I took on the role of an investigator, I found subjects from the community in which I was raised and named the project Understanding the Continuation of Female Genital Cutting in the United States among the Dawoodi Bohra Community. I disrupted the history of traditions my ancestors came from to ensure my story of undergoing FGC, which was, and is, the story of thousands of girls from Asian backgrounds, counted.

Research, I believed, could become the antidote to my curiosity. My research would not blame, but comprehend. There was a darkness that had formed in my mind over the years, a rationality I had developed through school, that wouldn't allow me to make sense of how inflicting pain on someone meant love. Those concepts were opposite, contradictory in nature, but had somehow been bridged together in the act of genital cutting.

I spoke to women who like me had grown up Dawoodi Bohra. I listened to them tell their stories of undergoing khatna, and felt a weight, a heavy burden, lift. Their stories were not always filled with disgust or hatred or anger at having to undergo it. Sometimes they spoke of the practice as needing to be continued. Every story was different, each woman behind the story unique. Linking us together was the piece of flesh that had been removed from us without our consent.

One woman spoke of the rage and betrayal she felt toward her mother, another persisted that khatna had to be done—it was mundane, like the occurrence of your period she said, and yet another touched upon the need for the diaspora to hold onto traditions more desperately than families in India. With each story, my knowledge gap grew smaller, light illuminated the darkness that drew my curiosity. Female genital cutting was not simply an act carried out by ignorant or uneducated people. It is what I now know to be a "social norm." An expectation overtly or covertly agreed to because the custom has been in place for decades, maybe even centuries. Something akin to removing your shoes before you enter a mosque or temple, because if you didn't remove your footwear, you would be disrespecting the purity of the religious buildings, you would be viewed as disrespectful. By not removing your shoes, you would be breaking a social norm.

But FGC was a social norm that needed to be broken. More stories needed to be told, more than my project, a master's thesis, allowed. Another inkling was born in me—a seed that would grow for years and years underground until it took the form of what the world knows as Sahiyo. The word means "friend" in Bohra Guajarati. Sahiyo is also the name of an organization I and four other women cofounded because each of us had felt the pain of khatna. Two of us had undergone it as children; two were spared but their families' members—one's mother and another's older sister—had not been; the last was not raised in the Dawoodi Bohra community, but she, as a South Asian, understood the complexity of harmful traditions and created the first ever documentary on FGC in India.

We each felt the same conflict in speaking up about the cutting. None of us wanted to shame those responsible for its continuation. We wanted to end the silence, the idea that it was taboo to discuss. We shared our stories; we encouraged other women to share their own stories. We harnessed the power of storytelling to illuminate the world to this problem. Together, we created a space where women who underwent FGC expressed their deepest feelings and healed through writing blogs, taking pictures, and producing videos, which we then disseminated via the Internet.

That clinical first response, the way I pursued academia to help me contemplate this question of love and pain, is what led me onto this path, and reflecting now, I understand that engaging academia is how I healed, and how I forgave those who had bestowed this tradition on me without my consent. Understanding the why for how an act of genital cutting could be done out of love also connected me to other women who like me wanted FGC to stop. And it was the collecting of their stories, first for my thesis, now for Sahiyo, that made me bolder and encouraged me to speak up and against the history I fell into. In August 2016, for the first time ever, I came out on video to ABC News about undergoing FGC.

My mother saw the segment.

My father saw it.

Everyone I knew saw it.

Everyone my parents knew saw it.

I should have felt elated—finally my story counted—yet despair rose instead.

That August, besides being on national news, I graduated from an MFA program. My parents flew from California to Massachusetts to hear me read out loud the short stories I had written and to see me walk across a stage to receive my diploma. On a weekend that was supposed to be celebratory, what is burned firmly in my memory is not my graduation or the culmination of two years of hard work but the visceral anger on my mother's face the day I picked my parents up at Logan airport. Her eyebrows were squeezed together to form a crease, her nose flared, and her eyes narrowed in on my presence. She demanded my father lecture me on the wrongdoing I had involved myself in by sharing my FGC story with the media. I was reminded of the 16-year-old I once was, the teenager who fought with her mother, because that is what mothers and teenage daughters do. I wondered how I would survive the weekend with her by my side.

She surprised me.

Over the course of those next few days, my mother's tone shifted, the tight lines on her face softened, and curiosity, a need to understand (a feeling I recognized too well), emerged from her. She asked me, "Why did you have to say you had it done? Why couldn't you say you knew it happened because of your research?"

Her body relaxed, the defensive stance in which she had held her shoulders upright for more than a day gave way to the comfort of her hotel armchair. The shape of her mouth turned neutral, as if the corners were perplexed whether they should turn upside-down in a frown or upwards in a smile, but in their neutrality, they could invite me into conversation. I saw her eyes withdraw to the ground, then up at me. I understood her real concern.

She once told me that when it came time to have my khatna done, my aunt came along because she, my mother, was afraid to see me writhing in pain. She was afraid she would be unable to hold down her seven-year-old child through the ordeal. In the hotel room, her body told me she was still afraid. Perhaps also ashamed of the pain she inflicted on me. I thought about the silence that all women who undergo khatna are trained to follow. How we are told to keep quiet, warned never to tell another soul, not even the men in our families. I wondered if my mother's small acknowledgment of the hurt she inflicted on me was a familiar feeling to the rest of the Dawoodi Bohras. Could that be why, for centuries, women were taught not to discuss it out loud? To keep it secret was to admit we inflicted pain on one another. To remain quiet was to hide the truth, to keep the pain, the regret my mother felt, hidden.

In that hotel room, for the first time I spoke words my mother needed to hear. "I'm not mad at you," I told her. I shared my story not to reflect poorly on her upbringing of me, but because I wanted women like me to find their voices and to let the truth surface. I no longer wanted my ancestors, and other Dawoodi Bohra women, to be unacknowledged statistics. Our stories needed to be part of the collective consciousness. In the end, I shared my story because the shortfalls of academia are what motivated me to push myself, push my peers, push my community, push my critics, push my culture, push my forebears, push my instincts and beliefs, and fears. To take a risk. To change. I told my mother that I broke the silence and disrupted the history from which I was born so that I may share my story and the stories of other women like me so that together we could prevent the pain from continuing to the next generation.

STRATO-CHRISTMAS '66

Jimmy E. Searles

December 1966. I'm your basic 10-year-old comic-book-loving, baseball-card-collecting Ohio boy, gearing up for Christmas and looking forward to my holiday vacation, being freed from the rotten school prison I've been held in since early September.

I'm holed up in a town called Diamond Lakes, Ohio, a has-been remnant of what was once a quaint early 1920s summer resort area outside of Dayton built among ponds and small lakes linked together by a series of canals.

There are a number of man-made islands with gazeebos and clubhouses, but you have to be a dues-paying member of Diamond Lakes to be able to use the facilities.

There is also a crappy used-to-be beach area with a concession stand for swinging summertime fun. My family has no access to any of it because the old man feels he hasn't climbed the ladder high enough and doesn't want to put out the dough for something he has no use for.

I don't know how to swim—and look pathetically scrawny and washed-out in a bathing suit anyway—so why put my life in jeopardy of being teased and humiliated by the neighborhood bullies hanging out just a-waiting for an easy mark like me to straggle by?

Wintertime is my thing and ice-skating is my game, especially when out of school for the holidays. If it's a decent winter and the ice is thick enough to hold my skin and bones, most evenings and weekends are spent ice-skating from lake to lake, up one canal and down another.

I can skate as well as anybody, and on virgin ice with the wind at my back, it's like I'm riding an air cushion, effortless as a feather across motionless blue glass, pushed along by a gentle breeze.

I skate for hours some days if the weather holds. I'm in it for the freedom. Many of my pals are only into ice skating to play hockey. Hockey never caught on with me for it ultimately seemed to lead to the real goal of boys wanting to beat other boys with hockey sticks, to play war with each other, wrestle around, be the tough guy.

Groups of teen boys and girls huddle along the banks of the main lakes, warming themselves by huge fires at the numerous beer-fueled skating parties, none of which I'd yet been invited to in fear I might keep hanging around and eventually cramp their style or embarrass my older brother and sister whom sooner or later I would surely spot imbibing among the crowd as I glide by in the winter shadows.

I prefer to skate alone most times anyway with nothing but the sound of my blades cutting through on fresh ice, knowing I am the first explorer of this newly created terrain. My mind roams free as I ramble and I am at one with the solitude, something I rarely have at home sharing a tiny bedroom in a tiny house with my pain-in-the-butt brother.

My best pal, Lenny, skates with me every once in a while but he is sickly, so his doting mother rarely gives in and lets him live outside his bubble. They are Methodists, Lenny tells me, and every night the family gets together and reads Bible passages to each other. I don't know what Methodist means. I have never stepped inside a church, not once.

One of the best things I like about hanging with Lenny is that I beat the crap out of him every time we play Monopoly. At times we are capable of filling a long summer day just playing one game after another where I win over and over. I want to walk away after hours of beating his butt then he begs me to go another round. I take everything from him, even his pride, every last dollar and property but he wants more, one more chance to win at last. I should let him win every now and then but I don't have it in me.

We have known each other since before I can remember, and we've had our ups and downs. Like during the last presidential election between Johnson and Goldwater. His churchy parents backed Republican Goldwater and mine were straight-up Johnson fans. Lenny and I were fed the propaganda daily from both camps knowing our respective parents had to be on the right side of things. Whatever that was, for neither one of us at eight years old had a clue to what any of it meant.

But boy we would stake our claims to righteousness and argue for hours spouting out the points of views of our parents that had been spoon-fed to us, both of us not being the wiser.

Now that Johnson is president I shove it up into his face every chance I get.

Lenny and I talk up our Christmas wish lists. He wants a brand new Monopoly game, one that will lean in his favor, a kind of voodoo Monopoly board I guess.

"That's it? Not a bike or a go-cart?" I ask him.

I know what I want, a brand new pair of ice skates and a couple of model cars to build, like a '55 Chevy Nomad wagon or a '53 Studebaker.

A new banana seat for my bike would be sweet but not as sweet as a new television for me and my brother's bedroom. Also, I want strings for the one-string acoustic guitar I found in someone's trash by the side of the road last summer, for I've had the bug of being a rock and roller lately but it looks stupid doing it with only one string.

Actually, I've had the bug a couple of years, having caught it on a cold February night in 1964.

"I want everybody here tonight to watch these Beatle boys," Dad ordered.

"The world's goin' crazy for these long-haired kids, it's a big deal, big news in the music world. Some are sayin' it will put Elvis outta business."

The old man liked big deals, whether it was NASA blasting rockets into space, H-bomb tests, or marches on Washington. If Walter Cronkite says pay attention, Pops was on top of the situation.

"She loves you yeah, yeah, yeah!" they belted out. And the "yeah, yeah, yeahs" floored me, setting off an alarm in my head that I heeded right away, saying, "Roll over, Elvis, and give the old-timers the news." Long hair combed down to their eyebrows, girls and boys screaming, Rickenbacker guitar, Hofner bass, exotic, an atomic engine blasting us out of the past and slam bang into the future.

Trying in desperate vanity the next morning before school to comb my butch-waxed flat-top down to look like John Lennon's mop-top Beatle cut was no deal. My pals were asking me why I was going with a dumb Jerry Lewis Nutty Professor look.

Playing "Louie, Louie" on my one and only string while I stood in front of my mirror as the platter spun was my newest thrill. I wanted to be a Beatle, or Dave Clark . . . even Herman the Hermit for crying out loud.

I wanted all the latest records I could get my hands on and I wanted them all the time. I saw myself on stage: a cool Roy Orbison with his coal-black Ray-Bans singing about blue bayous and pretty women.

Pipe dreams at best, I somehow figured out in my preteen brain, so eventually I drifted back to my usual interests of baseball, comics, and skating—pre-Beatles stuff.

Old One String, the name I'd given the guitar, called to me every once in a while. I'd notice her in the corner covered in a coat of dust and feel guilty, pull her onto my lap, and make the best one-string riff I could. My old man would tease me about the guitar.

"You know that thing would work better with six strings."

At some point, maybe about a year ago, our family began to resemble the prime time television shows' families, or slightly just shy of the Joneses down the street. In summer at just about lunch time, Mom would have me walk with her about a mile out of town to Elmer's Creek, which meandered through the cornfields, to wait for Dad to come sliding up in his company Jeep to grab a quick smooch and a sack lunch from Momma.

Swooping in like Errol Flynn returning from an African safari, he rode his World War II jeep like a bucking bronc, further convincing me he had no need for nightly television shows the likes of *Combat* and *The Rat Pack*. Daddy was living it.

Dad was a Cub Scout Master around the time I was eight years old, leading the charge with my brother in tow, Boy Scout number one. As a family we were showing up at community parties like graduation ceremonies and big-wig sweet sixteen birthday galas where Mom would bring the potato salad that she agonized over the night before, wondering if it would suit the neighborhood in-crowd.

Summers were dream-filled with ice cream trucks, milk deliveries, bookmobiles, camping trips, kite-flying, comic books, and endless days of bike-riding and baseball.

Dad would even take my brother and me along with him to pick up his boss's business partners in places like Detroit and Chicago on his boss's private plane, a DC-3 tail dragger equipped with a fully stocked bar, living room furniture instead of your standard seats, and, more importantly, drawers filled with every type of candy under the sun. We were lower middle class for sure but the future looked bright.

Before he began his journey to be the best tie-wearing, well-respected man about town he could be, back in the late forties and early fifties the old man played guitar and sang in hillbilly bands throughout Ohio, Michigan, and Kentucky. He rode around on motorcycles, and on the weekends for fun he'd race an old '34 Ford coupe he'd hopped up at the Shady Bowl racetrack.

I heard the stories over and over from aunts and uncles of what a guitar-slinging hellcat he was, who on more than a few nights ended up fighting his way out of a bar being accused rightly or not of enticing the lusts of wives and girlfriends of drunken barflies.

Mom, having moved from the hollers of Kentucky, quickly adapted to big city, factory work and to taking in the dive bar nightlife on the weekends. Tough joints with names like the Ring Bar or the Downtime in the days before I plopped into the scene. Daddy met Momma in a bar, starting with her buying drinks to be placed on the stage aside his honky-tonk hardwood floor stomping and time-keeping cowboy boot. As fate would have it, the stars twinkled over Ohio, and in time cowboy Pa and honky-tonk angel Ma hooked up in hillbilly fashion to form a more perfect union.

He quit playing the year I was born, naming me after a steel guitar player in the last band he was in, and then quickly settled into a more domestic life with Mother. Wanting to do the right thing and provide a steady life, Dad worked his way up to a supervisory position with a major homebuilder, hitting the gas on a moving-on-up lifestyle. We went on vacations to Florida a few years in a row and would film the events on our brand new 8-millimeter color home movie camera.

About the time I hit nine years of age I began to notice Daddy-o's lust for that country beat. It was all he could do to contain himself when the newest George Jones album hit the racks. Adapting to being Mr. Responsible during the work week, by Friday afternoon when that paycheck was handed off to him by the boss he was ready to roll. First stop after cashing in was Flip Side Records, the local disc-o-rama catering to the needs of the record junkies.

Mom would complain he was wasting hard-earned grocery money, but only to us kids, and then in a whisper so as not to rile who she sometimes called Mount Eruptis because of his sometimes, of late, short fuse.

No woman was going tell jeep-driving, gear-jamming Papa how or what to spend his hard-earned dough on. Sometimes, though, almost as half of an excuse to be a good dad thinking of his adoring son, he'd slip in the newest Teen Beat 45 rpm record, just for me.

Around that time, usually on Sundays, our home took on a spiritual feel because Dad would play one record after another, religiously, from Lefty Frizzell to Woody Guthrie to Louie Armstrong. You had to be quiet around the house on that day, respectful of his one day a week to reconnect with his true love, or suffer the consequences.

That was then and this is now and Christmas Eve is colder than any I can remember as my older brother and I lie head-to-toe under fine handmade quilts, presents from our Kentucky mountain grandmother, watching some has-been holiday movie on our crappy black and white TV with the rigged-up tinfoil rabbit ears. I am wired, hyped out of my head, and brother is trying to sleep.

Christmas is still a gas to me as he tosses and turns with indifference to the significance of what the next morning brings. He is older, wiser, and I think slightly drunk from knocking the brewskies back at the latest skating party. I try to ignore him and focus instead on how our house is the best decorated on the block.

Dad takes pride in his Christmas decorations. Outside a lit-up life-size Santa sits in his souped-up twinkle-twinkle sleigh led by the reindeer that have all been made up to look like Rudolph with red blinking noses. Lights are draped over every bush and pine tree in our yard and most of the house. A soft blanket of snow completes my Yuletide vision, insuring the perfect Christmas just like the one I used to know. Or the one Bing Crosby used to know.

Christmas morn and I am roused out of bed in a manner I am unaccustomed to.

"You ever gonna get up, boy?" Dad grunts, thus ejecting me from the cockpit of the P-51 fighter I was piloting in my dreams, just as I was poised to swoop down over Berlin and free the world of Hitler.

"You're always the first up on Christmas morn, knockin' around the kitchen, rattling pots 'n' pans, wakin' the rest of us up, but TODAY you decide to sleep in."

Excited as I'd ever seen him I feel the grasp of his huge construction worker hand wrapped around my little boy wrist jerking me in one motion from the bed, and before I know it I'm standing in the hall just around the corner from the living room, where I am told to stay until he gives the word for me to enter.

I smell a rat, and as the fog lifts I realize from the muffled giggles and whisperings that my whole family was already in the living room obviously enjoying some kind of secret doings that only a Super Christmas could generate.

"You ready, Jake?"

Am I ready? What the hell is going on here? Can I pee first?

"Get your ass on in here then," Dad says as I round the corner in slow motion dream steps, parting the Technicolor sea of Christmas reds and greens, simultaneous split-screen views of frosty windows, grinning mom, wide-eyed brother and sisters. Beautifully wrapped presents piled high around the tinseled six-foot Christmas tree guarded by a fortress wall of whiskey bottles in decorative boxes with exotic names like Black Velvet and Canadian Club, gifts from Dad's work associates, his boss, and his 450-pound best pal, Herman the Cadillac dealer.

Momentarily I realize how I love looking at whiskey Christmas gift boxes and find myself comforted by the images. I notice the TV is on with the sound turned down showing *Miracle on 34th Street*. I take in the seasonal scenes depicted on the different styles of wrapping paper. Snowmen riding sleds down snow-covered hills, wearing multicolored scarves and black top hats all beautiful, all hiding the jewels of our Santa dreams and in the thick of it I hear the other end of the tunnel voice of Dad.

"Well, do ya like your present or don't ya?"

I don't see the forest for the trees, for right between the Christmas tree and the stereo, bathed in a heavenly light beautifully displayed inside the crimson felt splendor of an opened-up guitar case, stands a Fender Stratocaster guitar plugged into a brand spanking new Sears Silvertone amplifier!

I look up at Dad, then to Mom, back to the guitar, to Dad again, his eyes sparkling snowflake diamonds beaming tinsel town pride in full knowledge of his superior gift-giving abilities.

I struggle to process the situation and am overwhelmed. Dad is Superman, he is THE Santa Clause who along with Mom just gave me not just any gift but a cool rock and roll present that was a green light saying run, run, Rudolph, this is your rocket outta here, past Lenny and Brian and little Katie from across the street, who will all most likely end up installing radiators in the local GM plant the rest of their livelong days settling for what life dishes out to them.

I begin to openly, violently, sob as though my own mother died and was dramatically brought back to life in front of my eyes while cradling the smooth curves and sleek maple neck of the Strat ever so gently for fear of hurting or breaking this object of beauty. Reverently I turn the glistening ivory guitar keys and press gently down on the string bending whammy-bar to create, with volume up to full, a primal noise likely never heard at 7:00 am on Christmas morning on Pine Road in Diamond Lakes, Ohio.

I thought the 12-gauge shotgun present two Christmases back was the best gift I would ever get . . . yet I didn't cry one tear over that one because of course if you get a gun for a present it's probably best not to start weeping, especially if you're wearing a coon skin cap and holding a box of shells.

I practice every day through the first couple of months into the new year, desperate in my attempts to learn complete songs or riffs from some of my favorites like the Keith Richards one on "Satisfaction" or the chords to "Help Me, Rhonda," the first song I ever danced with a girl to the summer before.

Some tunes come easy, mostly the country ones Dad is teaching me. When I'm busy with other distractions like skating or school, Dad picks more and more on the guitar, more than eager at times to show me chords and how to finger pick, yet it is obvious he is a pro and I am beside myself not having ever really known or paid attention to what a gifted musician he was.

There are days I get home from school or from playing outside and find Dad locked in his bedroom jamming out on my guitar, and at times it would be several days before the guitar and amp would mysteriously reappear in my room.

I notice in just the space of a few months I'm losing interest in some of my old desires like baseball and model car building. I fret over important issues like how do I get the money for a new pair of Beatle boots, ribbed corduroy jeans, and a matching mod paisley shirt, the kind of outfit required if you want to impress someone like maybe the cute little brown-eyed buggaboo daughter of the couple that just moved in down the block named Diane whom within a few weeks would become my main 11-year-old squeeze.

It's a cold-ass March day as I stagger home from playing flag football with my pals to a house filled with musicians—a full band, a steel guitarist and fiddle player all backing up Daddy, who's wailing away on some weird old country song as beehive-haired Mom sways, beer in hand, to the old-time rhythms being laid down. The music is not my cup of meat but I sit listening in silent awe, marveling at the level of their talent, still dismayed by my ignorance of Dad's abilities in music.

Time is a freight train barreling down the track, with the weeks of 1967 piling up fast. It's getting to the point of having to practically beg Dad to borrow the guitar so I could practice or at least have it in my room where it gave me comfort just knowing it was beside my bed at night.

It appears he has completely confiscated my guitar although I know not to make an issue of it. I could practice on it some, he says, but have to be careful not to break any strings because they are expensive. Somehow he had lost his job as construction foreman and had to take a part-time job as a bulldozer operator.

Another thing I asked Momma about was what happened to Daddy's flat-top haircut. It came out of nowhere, a black-as-coal piled high mop of greased back hepcat hair complemented by carefully groomed sideburns Elvis would die for.

Everything is groovy, Mom informs me, because he's going to play music with his band in bars around town to supplement his income and most times she would accompany him for support, which led to the bottom line of my older brother and sister being in charge of me and our four-year-old sister on many Friday and Saturday nights.

I complain off-handedly to Dad about his confiscation of my Strat, but only in a way so as to insure my well-being, because if I were to cross the piss-off-Dad line I might wake up in the morning to find my precious Fender lying beside the bed in a pile of splinters with a can of lighter fluid sitting beside it and a note informing me I was grounded for a month.

But fortune smiles on me, for I still have my old acoustic and in a rare moment of feeling my pain, Dad sprang for some gut strings so I would have something to practice on. And practice I am, learning as best I can songs like "Light My Fire" by the Doors and "Do You Believe in Magic" by the Loving Spoonful, and all the while life is changing right under my nose.

I fall head over knees for my brown-eyed girl Diane as Lenny and I hang out less than ever through no fault of his. It's just I'm meeting new pals and they, like me, are locked away in their bedrooms, awake way past bedtime resting needles ever so lightly onto records with the sound down to barely audible so as not to cause a fuss, checking out the newest hip sounds.

Like "Freak Out" by this scary-looking bunch of longhairs called the Mothers of Invention, one of the records my brother brought home though nary an interest had he in the buried treasure embedded in the grooves of the black vinyl. He bought records just to have them around to impress the neighborhood girls he was constantly trying to lure into what he thought was his own little love pad, our bedroom.

Lately the old man's working construction jobs a couple of days a week at best. Money is tight and the rent always late. Mom does the job of an economist cutting grocery coupons, spending only what was needed to get by yet sits in quiet desperation of wanting to work, go out and find a job, but daddy-o will have none of that. She doesn't have a driver's license and Dad sees no point in a housewife driving—would end up being nothing but trouble. Mom said the other day he's just afraid she'd run off on him. He came near to punching her for that remark.

She is drinking more than ever, especially on the few days Dad goes into work, starting about ten minutes after the school bus has picked me up, and is usually sloshed by the time I get home in the afternoon. Her driving around drunk without a license would not be the best idea.

I learn most of this from brother and sister side talk. I find out where Mom has taken to hiding her beer inside the tub of our 1920s wringer washer that sits in the utility room beside my bedroom. The washer Dad bought on the payment plan from Shorty, the creepy, toothless gimpy dwarf who owns a local fishing pay lake nearby and has a side business selling used appliances.

My bedroom is a cinder block room that used to be a garage although the genius who made it into a bedroom failed to install heating ducts from the main house so the only way it could be heated was to leave the kitchen door open to let some heat drift through the utility room and hopefully enough would filter into our garage bedroom to warm the concrete floor covered with oil stains. Dad had big plans at one time to remodel our bedroom, but that was before Strat.

"Construction just don't pay in the winter," says the old man coming home early on payday with little to show for his toil, sharing the news the heat will be turned off for a few days due to lack of back payments to the home heating oil company.

Miraculously though, Father found a way to buy an expensive rhinestone-studded wagon wheel saguaro cactus jacket so loud even the famous guy who designs country music star duds, Nudie, would surely approve. Dad became the glistening crystal ball king of the lonesome hillbilly troubadours, standing center stage, making the old Chevrolet set squeal with delight when he whipped out the Hank Williams song "I'm So Lonesome I Could Cry" right before closing time at Dave's Whiskey Barn.

When not at work, Dad and Strat become inseparable. If he isn't practicing solo, he has the boys in the band hanging and jamming with him. Guys with names like "Curley" Bill Jones, a fiddle player friend of his from the old days and glorious drunkard that many a Sunday mornings I had to step over on my way into the living room since he'd passed out there at the break of dawn. Other players came and went but Curley hung until the end, and I never heard a better fiddle player since then.

An older cousin named Ronnie from Dad's side of the family that I have never heard of shows up one day. He's in his mid-thirties and plays what they call a pedal steel guitar. He has a lisp and kind of long hair and makes the funniest faces as he hits certain notes, kind of like a fly's buzzing around his nose and he can't swat at it. He's a nice guy but Dad makes fun of him. I like that Ronnie brings a little hipness into the mix, otherwise lacking in hillbilly heaven, by suggesting Dad and the band cover the Beatles song "Norwegian Wood."

Sure enough, last Friday I came home from school and within half a block recognized that song wafting down the street, stunned to walk in and find my old man wailing away on a Beatles song although he was doing the Waylon Jennings version because if ole Waylon thinks it's all right to play some hippie music, then he could too.

My older brother, sister, and I are learning to appreciate the positive effects of our disintegrating so-called normal family structure. When Dad's home these days he's usually edgy and doesn't go for small talk. If you want trouble he knows how to give and take it. We can plainly see that straight family life is beginning to bore him and unless Mom is drinking she's usually in a foul mood also. So, we want them out, out on the town, in the bars, at a Love-In, a hoedown, wherever. We need room to move, sin, rebel rouse and they are in the way.

Oddly enough, Dad rarely drinks. His thing is "the broads" that Mom accuses him of chasing. He hates Mom's drinking and she hates his womanizing and his hatred, but they put up with each other because with him playing clubs that way they both get what they want, two tickets to paradise for different reasons.

Lately he's getting more and more gigs from local bars to country music festivals around the state. We love when he does the outdoor bigtime jamboree shows the best because usually the parents are gone for the weekend, which means brother, sister, and I have the run of the house by God, even the whole damn neighborhood, and all we have to care about for up to 48 hours is making sure our youngest sister, sweet Melissa, is fed and in bed early so the party can commence.

And commence it does. First up as soon as the tailfins of Dad's beat-to-hell 1957 Cadillac fade off down the road, I am in full trot hot to knock on girlfriend Diane's bedroom window, bargaining for another steamy smooch-smooch session inside the life-sized dollhouse in our backyard Dad made for Melissa two years back in his Boy Scout leader/My *Three Sons* period.

All the while brother Jeff and his pals hold court inside the house swilling beer and putting the make on local chicks. Sister Connie is hot to shoot off to her girlfriend's pad for some fingernail-painting or to meet up with motorcycle Bill of tight leather biker pantsuit fame and maybe hang at the local pool hall or ride off and jump some barrels on the outskirts of town.

The whole scene is becoming routine with my sibs and me, and clever we have become in knowing exactly when to be home from running the streets, aware of the closing time hours of whatever dive Dad and his band are playing in because we know for sure that Mom would want to hang till then, not wanting to give up on the golden 12-ounce swirl and making sure Dad came home with her instead of going off with some barroom honey.

I find out from insiders that well-to-do parents in the neighborhood—otherwise known as the ones who pay their mortgages, rent, and utility bills and have at least three color televisions in their homes—had become wary of my lifestyle.

I have become the target, I am told, of a blacklisting campaign designed to protect their sweet children from my cigarette-smoking, bad influence, young and tough ways as, one by one, sons and daughters throughout the community of well-wishers are being banned with threats of being grounded from coming over to my house or even hanging with me anywhere.

What few friends my parents have in the hood are dropping like flies too. As a family I reckon we are living in oblivion to the growing perception of the town folk that we are nothing but trouble and should be avoided.

I don't even care because I'm spending more time with my imaginary friends anyway, and I am not talking about little teddy bears or army men toys, no, no, I'm talking about the likes of Jimi Hendrix, who happens to play an exact copy of my Fender, or Beatle John Lennon, who is for sure the Walrus.

And then there are the other strong distractions for my already too fragile 11-year-old mind to soak in, like my growing fondness for down and out B-movies that usually have something to do with drug abuse or alcoholism. Movies broadcast late night Saturdays when Momma and Poppa are fast awake in some dive letting the good times roll, allowing me the time to imbibe in, without fear of retribution, sweet little films like *The Man with the Golden Arm*, *Let No Man Write My Epitaph*, or the feel-good movie of 1945, *The Lost Weekend*.

And through some kind of divine interference, a benevolent benefactor from the blackest of holes in the universe decides my education will not be complete without one of my brother's friends leaving a book by some old beatnik named Jack Kerouac called *On the Road* sitting on the kitchen table.

My fun times with Diane are fading as summer winds down. It's getting difficult to drum up ways to be together without her parents finding out she is looking for puppy love in all the wrong places, like in my sister's life-sized dollhouse. She's beginning to distance herself from me, which hurts so bad. So much so I have taken to walking up and down in front of her house with my transistor radio turned up to ten every time they play the new hit Stevie Wonder song "I Was Made to Love Her," but to no avail.

I believe in magic but the magic appears to be drifting away. And last night at the skating rink when they played our song, "Light My Fire," Diane roller-skated right over my heart by looping hand-in-hand around the rink with Larry "Slimy" Simes, the dorkiest of the rotten lousy dorks.

It's getting to the point the only time Mom and Dad aren't fighting are the hours right before it's time for them to hit the road to another joint. I love those times.

The anticipation of our emancipation for the evening is usually ushered in by the house-filling odor of over-applied Hai Karate cologne, a signal to all of us wanting freedom that things are going as planned and his gig is a go. The wafting stench of cheap perfume Mom has taken to slapping on in extreme lately also confirms that there is no fear of cancelation, no chance of the awful reality of having "them" home with us to stifle all intended acts of rebellion we look forward to that evening.

As invigorating as those sacred moments are, it's all evened out by the pre-dawn, pre-hangover misery when they come home with Mom stewed to the gills, pissed perhaps justly so from one too many nods and winks in Dad's direction by bar gals hoping for a chance to ride on his hell-bound train.

And Dad beside and outside himself with a building, slow-burning rage over the perceived advances and leers of hopped-up hillbillies looking for action with his once-doting wifey as she, having been freed by the effects of alcohol, shook and shimmied on the beer-stained hardwood floor, and in his mind leading the men on. Mesmerizing in her blue sequined mini-dress, beehive hairdo swaying like a skyscraper in an earthquake, receiving the adoring attention of neglected automotive workers who believe it when Tammy Wynette sings your good girl's a-gonna go bad and be the swingiest swinger that you ever had cha cha cha.

Mom and Dad eventually make the long ride home unflinching and steadfast in their loathing of one another, coming through the front door in a tidal wave of hatred overflowing into a whirling dervish of violence, shaking the foundations of our slipping-away life, waking us kids from our sweet dreams as my brother, worried for Mom's safety, bolts from bed and I follow, to witness his valiant attempt to stop the brutality by bringing down a man twice his size.

Maybe it's because they are just wearing themselves out or they overhear something being muttered by someone on high that they might want to cool it for a while on the knock-down drag-outs, but for whatever reason about two weeks before school is to start there is some kind of secret truce signed.

Dad all of a sudden wants to do more family-type things and first on his list is to take Mom and us kids to our first drive-in movie experience.

Now we're talking. So . . . what's on tap daddy-o? A Disney film perhaps? A western? Oh, oh, yes I see . . . yes . . . a biker movie called *The Wild Angels*. Doesn't sound like your typical kid fair to me but who am I to complain?

If ever there was a movie to fuel this rebel without a pause it was *The Wild Angels*.

From the first vrooooom kick-start of the motorcycle engine to the razor sharp chainsaw fuzz distortion guitar coming from Davie Allan & The Arrows' song "Blues Theme" that opens the film, the guitar sound sliced through the core of everything phony, leaving television, homework, baseball cards, model rocket–building Cub Scouts behind in the dust of the dirt road that led out of the Skyborn Drive-In on that hot August night.

Lord have mercy, I am grinding to get home when the show is over and swipe the Fender back from Dad, plug in, and find that magical fuzz . . . when through the fog of pre-teen angst Dad's voice interrupts with a stern warning.

"I don't want you getting any wild ideas or being influenced by watching that movie, son, you hear?"

"Yeah, sure, Dad," I say, knowing full well I am already sitting in first class on a hell-bound train.

Before I fall into bed I take my Levis jacket and cut the sleeves off, pinning on what war medals I've bought over the years from the general surplus store, knowing I look just like Peter Fonda, the star of the biker movie.

By the end of the week I find an old bike put out with somebody's trash, cut the front forks off, and retrofit them onto my bike, giving it that wild chopper look I so desperately crave, allowing me the opportunity to form my own bike gang consisting of four others that lasts about a week, but what a week that was, baby.

Early September, back in school and I am more outcast than ever. I have nothing in common with the boys talking about old-time campy days on soft and easy summer Vacation Street or the precious-faced Barbie doll gals drooling over pictures of Monkee Davey Jones on the cover of *Teen Beat* magazine.

Few are interested or maybe they are in fear after hearing about my adventures during the so-called summer of love, one that culminated with another family outing of cultural import by going to the Demolition Derby at Kil-Kare Speedway. It was there where I had the privilege of witnessing an unassuming lady sitting unawares 20 feet away in the bleachers get ambushed by three gals with green in their eyes and tar and feathers in their hands. Within mere seconds blood flowed into the grooves of the metal benches in my direction. Somehow during the melee it was pieced together said unassuming lady was charged with messing around with one tar lady's man and was getting her just reward.

I dread the day I have to stand in front of the class for "what I did on summer vacation." I know I'll have to make something up.

From here to eternity is the time leading up to the Christmas break. Dad's still playing the bars and Mom is hanging around the washtub more than ever. The fights continue but the intensity has died down to a degree.

In a weird kind of shift, Dad has become downright glum, which is odd for him because one of the few times a year you can count on him to be a little upbeat is the holidays.

He is decorating for sure but this year is different.

This year Daddy is having a sad-as-hell blue Christmas with blue bells hanging from blue ceilings and blue garlands around blue windows, blue icicles dripping from a blue-tinseled tree as "Blue Must Be the Color of the Blues" and "Blue Christmas" ring out forlornly from the worn-out stereo purchased back in his father knows best days.

And let's not forget that sadder than sad tearjerker of a holiday song, "Blue Christmas Lights" by Buck Owens, spilling into my slowly being corrupted 11-year-old ears as I stare out my frost-covered unheated bedroom window watching sad, flickering reflections of outside blue lights dancing around the snowdrifts.

I feel aged in my soul, older than I should with a sadness I can't seem to shake. I long for my beautiful Strat and the sunlit Christmas morning of a year ago when the future couldn't have appeared brighter.

I mourn over Diane, the first girl that ever kissed me, who said beautiful tender things about me as her eyes, eyes that contained the entire universe of shimmering possibility, lulled me into a false, sweet comfort.

Now gone forever as far as I know, Diane having moved away just last week, disappearing like a thief in the night to heaven knows where on a day I was home from school death-sick, throat-swollen fever high piled under quilts to keep from freezing, for the heat had been turned off yet again from lack of payment.

And that was the same day Walt Disney died.

As I peer out the frosty window into the dead winter night, the sad blue world surrounding me makes me wonder what or who on earth triggered Dad's descent into the sad blue world he created. I figure from all the crazy screaming matches I have witnessed between him and Mom more than likely an outside source, one with heartbreaking intentions.

A sweater, flannel shirt, the new Stones album, and a new pair of used ice skates are my presents for Christmas 1967. The heating bill was paid so my room has been relatively warm for at least 3 of the 12 days of Christmas.

Pulling on my flannel shirt, my new sweater, and three pairs of socks, I grab my skates and walk down the hall past my parents' bedroom. I pause for just a moment noticing in the corner of the room a now banged-up 1957 Fender Stratocaster leaning against a frayed beer-and-cigarette stained Sears Silvertone amplifier.

I reflect momentarily on the joy I felt a year ago the moment I realized it was my present. On how I knew that moment would last forever, then finding out real quick nothing lasts forever.

Throwing my skates, tied together by the laces, over my shoulder I start my walk down the street toward the lake from my ramble shamble shack of a home. An icy gray fog permeates the air as I walk by Lenny's house, momentarily pausing, briefly having the urge to knock on his door for the first time in months just to see how he's doing.

Through the parted curtains of their kitchen, I see the rosy glow of Lenny's mother in early morning winter breakfast-making mode. She wears a tasteful Christmas tree apron, serenely at the stove in a life of stability and security.

Should I? I decide it's best to move on.

I gently, quietly slip onto the blue glass of the frozen pond and glide easily past the upscale homes that line the shores. Saturday morning breakfasts mixed with fireplace aromas piping out of chimneys fill the crystal metallic air and bring me joy.

I'm flying fearlessly now across the deepest part of the lake with the wind at my back, pushing me without effort straight into the New Year. A song rattles around my brain and without warning I find myself whistling an old-timey tune Daddy likes to sing called "Take Your Tomorrow (and Give Me Today)."

EIGHT STEPS DOWN
Steven Fromm

Dawshinski couldn't shake Whispering Smith. He hadn't worked the court beat for six years, but it didn't matter. Maybe it was trust. Dawshinski had never burned Whispering Smith. It had nothing to do with ethics. Whispering Smith was safe because Dawshinski had no idea who he was, though he had a general idea by following a simple chain of deduction: Whispering Smith worked somewhere in the courthouse. He was probably mid-level civil service. He'd probably been doing the same job for decades and was bored as hell.

And one other thing. He whispered his tips over the phone.

"Times," Dawshinski said into the phone. There was a pause.

"Walter Nero." It came out like a hoarse, breathy exhalation. They'd dropped cordial phone pleasantries long ago.

"What about him?"

"Indictment's coming down."

Dawshinski reached for his pen and pad.

"On Wally Nero?"

"That's the word."

"What's it involve?"

"Sketchy. Think it's sex-related."

"Sex-related? How do you know?"

"Feels sex-related."

"How can an indictment feel sex related?"

"Got instincts. Just like you."

Dawshinski didn't answer. Maybe Whispering Smith had instincts, but Dawshinski had no such illusions. Everything pretty much came down to an educated guess, which is a sober version of a lucky shot.

"When's it coming?"

"DA's gonna make an announcement. Soon. Maybe tomorrow."

"Anything else?"

"Maybe you want me to write it for you?"

"How much you charge per word?"

There was a pause, one more breathy exhalation, and then the line went dead.

"Who was that?" Doyle asked. He sat at a desk pressed up against the front of Dawshinski's in the cramped newsroom. He was in early, at least for him, which meant an all-nighter. His eyes were bloodshot, and he was sweating. He tended to sweat after a binge.

"Get lost on the way home?" Dawshinski asked.

"Fate led me down other paths."

"Fate can do that."

"Don't piss on fate," Doyle warned.

"Why not?"

"It usually pisses back."

"Some of us carry umbrellas."

"And some of us fools travel light," Doyle said. He was emptying a packet of sugar into black coffee. "So. Who was that?"

"Who was who?" Dawshinski asked.

"I heard 'indictment,'" Doyle said, searching for something on his desk. He picked up a red Bic pen and used it to stir his coffee.

"It was Whispering Smith."

Doyle looked at him, waiting. "You building suspense?"

"He says it's Wally Nero."

"Wally Nero? That boring putz?"

"That's what he says."

"No way," Doyle said, but not with much conviction. They both knew that Whispering Smith's batting average was pretty good. Even if he wasn't dead-on, there was almost always something to what he phoned in.

"He say what for?"

"Sex."

"Sex? What kind of sex?"

"Sex-related," Dawshinski said. "He said it feels sex-related."

"How does an indictment feel sex-related?" Doyle asked.

"When you figure it out, one of us will know," Dawshinski said.

"Don't try to be clever," Doyle said. "It aggravates my hangover."

Dawshinski didn't answer. He was thinking that the right thing to do was kick the tip to Dobson, the current courthouse reporter. Then again, Dawshinski wasn't much on doing the right thing. He didn't pretend to be above the petty competitiveness that made most journalists, in essence, a bunch of pricks. Plus, Wally Nero was a state assemblyman now, which put him squarely on Dawshinski's beat. And another thing. Nero and he were friends. Or at least as close to being friends as an officeholder can get with a reporter who covers him. It wasn't something Dawshinski liked to talk about. Reporters weren't supposed to be friends with people they covered. Then again, reporters did a lot of things they shouldn't do, including unethical friendships. No one seemed to care, least of all the reporters.

It was that timely fusion of knowing someone when they were no one, but still treating them with a cordial respect that slowly ripens into a sturdy friendship. It didn't hurt that they shared a few things in common: a passion for baseball, just about any film with Bogart in it, and The Who (the Keith Moon version). As is often the case in a small metro area with one dominant paper and a reasonably functional political machine, their careers intersected as they moved up. They first met when Nero was president of a school board that was part of Dawshinski's municipal beat, his first at the paper. Nero moved on to the township council, then to a spot on the county freeholder commission. After two years he graduated to a state Assembly seat, his bland Republicanism and spunky, two-child nuclear family helping him coast his way through a sprawling suburban election district that favored soothing, retro-Reagan chants of contained taxes, minimal government, law enforcement, and civic pride. His name was in the running for a vacant state Senate seat.

But their friendship was built on more than intertwining careers. When Nero's eight-year-old son was hospitalized with a ruptured appendix, Dawshinski showed up with a toy for the kid and consolation for Nero. When Dawshinski was in rehab, suspended from the paper and drifting through a gulag of group sessions, gallons of lousy coffee, and daytime TV, Nero showed up with a six-pack of ginger ale to watch the Yanks plow through Boston. It was those moments that transformed their interactions from something professional to personal, from strategic to organic.

"So," Doyle said, "what're you gonna do?"

"Call the DA's office."

Doyle didn't answer. He didn't have to. Calling the DA's office and asking about an impending indictment was akin to calling the Vatican and asking if the Pontiff wanted to play a round of golf before lunch.

"I guess I'm going to call Wally," Dawshinski finally said.

"And do what? Ask him if he's going to be indicted for something sex-related?"

"Not exactly," Dawshinski said. "I'll just call and say hello. Chat him up. See if anything pops."

"Right. You'll inquire about each other's weekends, maybe discuss the ballgame, and then he's gonna say, 'Oh. By the way. I'm getting indicted for solicitation.' Something like that?"

"Something like that."

"Don't you just love investigative journalism?"

"It has its charms."

He started dialing Nero's cell from his office phone, then hung up and used his cell. That way it wouldn't look like official business. Dawshinski didn't want to be thinking that way, but he had to. There were three rings, then voicemail picked up.

"Wally, buddy. Where you been? Give me a call back, dude." He put the phone down and looked at Doyle.

"Did I sound casual?"

"'Dude' was a bit much, but you passed the screen test. Now what?"

"I wait."

"Good idea. Hold onto the son-of-a-bitch until you know it can't be had, then lateral it to Dobson so he can flame out. It's win-win."

"That sounds pretty Machiavellian."

"Hey. Mac's my man."

"He woulda been big in this business."

"Woulda been publisher," Doyle observed, "maybe with Homer as his hatchet man."

"Homer?"

"Didn't Homer serve as his guide through the Circles?"

"That was Virgil."

"Virgil? You sure?"

"Positive."

"When did you last read the *Inferno*?"

"When I was drying out."

"The *Inferno* in rehab. Is there something ironic about that?"

"Probably. Even though ironic is the wrong word. I also read *Moby Dick*."

"Another light-hearted romance."

"I coulda read some chick-lit. Maybe a memoir."

"Then you would've started drinking again," Doyle said, taking another loud slurp from his coffee.

Dawshinski's cell phone rang. He looked at the screen.

"It's him," he said.

"Jesus."

Dawshinski pressed talk. "Hello?"

"Dash?" Nero was one of the few people who called him that.

"Whattup, bud?" Dawshinski said. His voice cracked on "bud." Doyle winced.

"This and that," Nero said after a few moments of silence.

"I usually prefer 'this' in the morning, 'that' in the p.m."

There was no retort. Then he knew something was up. He and Nero almost always eased into a natural flow of meaningless bullshit that led nowhere. It wasn't supposed to. That was the pleasure of it. Dawshinski took another stab.

"Come to think of it, while I got you on the phone, you can settle something for me."

"Settle?"

"More of a trivia thing," Dawshinski said. "You being an Italian with a halfway decent education, I was wondering if you ever read Dante's *Inferno?*"

Doyle smiled between small sips of coffee. Nero didn't answer. Dawshinski decided to press ahead. He had no choice.

"My friend says it was Homer who led Dante through the Circles. I say it was Virgil. What say you?"

More silence. Dawshinski looked at Doyle, who gave him a shrug, then dumped another packet of sugar into his half-empty cup.

"Dash?" Nero asked.

"Yeah?"

"I have to go."

"Wally?"

"I have to go," he said.

"Sure, bud, but—"

The line went dead. Dawshinski put the cell phone back down on his desk.

"Well?" Doyle asked.

"It's true."

"Jesus H. You think?"

"That was Wally, but he wasn't there. You know what I mean?"

"No. But what're you gonna do?"

"Work it with Dobson. Unless you want in."

"Thanks, but no thanks," Doyle said. "It sounds too much like work."

The cell rang again. Dawshinski picked it up.

"Him again."

"Chatty guy."

Dawshinski pressed talk. "Hello?"

"Dash?"

"Hey, Wally. You okay?"

"Yes. No. Not really. You have a minute?"

"Two or three. What's up?"

"There're some issues. An issue."

Dawshinski waited for a beat. "Yes?"

"It's something I have to handle."

"What?"

"It's an issue. It involves a mistake."

"A mistake?"

"A mistake. Something's going to happen. I have to handle it."

"Handle it," Dawshinski repeated. He was trying to start a rhythm to coax the next sentence.

"A mistake," Nero said. "My mistake."

"What mistake?"

"A big mistake." His voice almost broke on "big." That's when Dawshinski knew for sure. Sex-related. Score another one for Whispering Smith.

"You want to meet up? Talk about it?"

Doyle winced again. Dawshinski didn't want to rush it, but he didn't know where else to go. There was another long pause. Nero was probably calculating the odds of Dawshinski calling the cops. If he was thinking halfway right, he knew it wouldn't happen.

"Well?" Doyle asked when Dawshinski hung up.

"We're going to meet."

"All this before the first cup of coffee. Where?"

"Motel Six."

"Which one?"

"Route 206 south. Room 223."

"He call anybody else?"

"Doubt it. I think he wants to come clean with someone he knows first. You know. Wants to hear how it sounds."

"A rehearsal."

"Something like that. And he shouldn't be alone."

"That doesn't sound good."

"I don't think much of anything's going to sound good today."

The Motel Six was two miles down, on his left. Dawshinski swung right into a jug handle, curved around, caught the green light, and crossed 206 into a huge asphalt parking lot that served as safe harbor for the constant fleet of 18-wheelers that came plying off the nearby New Jersey Turnpike. He drove past a small diner marooned in the middle of the lot. When he got close enough to the motel, he spotted a sign for rooms 220 to 250 with an arrow pointing left. He found a spot in front of the nearest stairwell and parked. There were only a few cars near the motel. Nero drove a dark blue Ford Explorer, but Dawshinski didn't see it. He climbed the stairwell, taking two steps at a time, then turned left when he hit the landing. Nero would be three doors in. Muffled TV noises came from 221. He thought he heard Fred Frawley's gravelly voice, then canned laughter. *I Love Lucy*. A woman's high-pitched laughter came from behind 222, followed by a sharp slapping sound and more playful laughter. When he got to 223 he stopped in front of the door, staring at the little peephole and wondering if Nero stood on the other side, staring back. He knocked softly on the door. Another slapping sound from 222. More laughter. A man's deep voice said something. Dawshinski knocked again, this time a bit harder. There was the scraping sound of a metal chain sliding and the single clack of a deadbolt. The door opened to reveal Wally Nero, bloodshot eyes blinking in the sudden sunlight, pudgy Wally Nero in a wrinkled, untucked white T-shirt, jeans and white socks, his thinning black hair ruffled and puffed by static charge.

"Dash," he said. It wasn't a greeting, just a flat word, as if he were objectively noting that Dawshinski had appeared at his door. He took one step to the side and motioned him in.

Dawshinski stepped into the room. Nero shut the door, flicked the deadbolt, and hooked the chain. The heavy drapes were closed. A dim lamp on the bedside table was on, along with the bathroom light in the back. As Dawshinski's eyes adjusted to the gloom his other senses took over. He picked up the usual cocktail of motel room odors: some kind of lemony cleaner and Windex tinged with a faint smell of leftover breakfast, something with sausage and eggs. The dark blue comforters on both double beds hadn't been turned down, but the one nearest the window was rumpled, its pillows mashed against the headboard. A TV on a long bureau to his left was on with the sound muted. CNN. A White House press conference. Nero walked back toward the bathroom. Dawshinski noticed the sink tap was running. Nero turned it off and came back into the room drying his hands with a white towel.

"You come alone?"

"Yes."

"Good. Thanks. Good."

He stood there with the towel bunched in his hands, not sure what to do next. He tossed the towel on the bed, then picked it up, folded it, and put it back down. He was all brittle movements, tense and quick. When he looked at Dawshinski, their eyes never quite met. He walked over to a small, round table to the left of the door, just in front of the window and cleared off McDonald's wrappings, an empty Oreo cookie package, and two empty bottles of Pepsi. After dropping them into a little plastic trash can under the table, he slumped into the chair facing the room, his back to the door. Dawshinski took off his jacket and slung it on the back of the remaining chair. He thought about taking out his recorder and notepad, but decided against it and sat down.

"You ever sleep here?" Nero asked.

"What?"

"Here. Did you ever sleep here?"

Dawshinski shook his head.

"It's an experience," Nero said, leaning back, hands in his lap. "I think there's a couple a few doors down. These sounds. I don't know what the hell's going on in there."

"We can only guess."

"I don't want to guess," Nero said. He almost smiled. "But somewhere around 3 a.m. or so, it really gets—what's the word? Peaceful. Even here. The trucker guys keep their rigs going in the parking lot sometime, but the rumble kind of settles into the background. Then there's the Turnpike. You can hear it from here. But it's not bad. It's the tires."

"The tires?"

"The truck tires on the road," Nero said. "There's this whining sound. You listen long enough, it sounds almost human or something. It's there, it fades. One after another. It's kind of lulling. I can almost sleep."

Dawshinski let him talk. Maybe it would relax him. Maybe it would relax both of them. There was more canned laughter from next door. Dawshinski looked at the TV. Syria again. Another round of bombing someone for something.

"You come alone?" Nero asked.

"You asked me that."

"Right. Yes. Alone. Tell anyone?"

"About what?"

"Where you are?"

"No. Yes. My boss," Dawshinski said. He'd let McRay, the ME, know what was going on before he left. He didn't mention Doyle. It would take too much explaining, and he wanted to keep things simple.

"What have you heard?"

"Not much," Dawshinski said. "There's an indictment. It's supposedly got your name on it."

"Anything else?"

"Just a guess."

"What's the guess?"

"It's sex-related."

Nero considered the words, his eyes straying for a moment to just over Dawshinski's head.

"Sex-related," he repeated. He was almost smiling.

"Is it?"

"That makes it sound like something it's not."

"What is it then?"

"Since we talked on the phone I've been thinking about how to tell you," Nero said. "I mean, if I tell it one way, it's sleazy. Another way it's too, I guess the word is clinical. Too clinical."

Gauging his message, a politician to the last, Dawshinski thought. He didn't say anything, figuring that if he sat there long enough, Nero would give it up.

"It's a woman."

"A woman?"

"Okay. Not a woman. Or not quite a woman."

"A girl?"

"Don't—" He snapped the word out. Their eyes met directly for the first time. He cleared his throat. "Don't call her a 'girl,'" he said softly. "You know. The sound of it."

"How old?"

"Sixteen."

"Sixteen," Dawshinski repeated.

"Almost seventeen," Nero said. He looked at Dawshinski for a long moment. It wasn't friendly. "Well. Fuckin' say something."

"Jesus, Wally."

Nero held his hands up, palms toward Dawshinski as if deflecting some kind of projectile. "I know. I know." He sunk deeper into this chair, his hands dropping back into his lap. The tension had eased. It was out now. Seventeen. Almost.

"How'd you meet?"

"During the primaries."

"Which ones?"

"Mine. The last one, when I beat that clown Hunter by what? Seventeen points. She was a volunteer." He smiled again. "She was doing it for school credit."

"I see," Dawshinski said.

"No, you don't," Nero said. "I mean, I can say it. But it's the kind of thing where even if you understand it, I don't think you'll admit it."

"Don't underestimate me," Dawshinski said.

"I'm not," Nero said. "That's why you're here." He took a deep breath and placed his hands on the table, palms pressing down. "From the very first I noticed it. Maturity's not the word. It's a horseshit word. It was some kind of weight she had. She had some kind of gravity. The way she carried herself. The way she looked at me. The way she talked. You see? Right there I knew she was special."

"I've run across a few," Dawshinski said, but Nero didn't seem to hear him.

"She kept turning up at all the functions," he said. "Fund-raisers, barbeques, youth rallies. We just started talking more and more. And there was this one moment, one moment in the middle of some bullshit conversation and I looked at her and she looked at me and I kept talking but I wasn't really keeping track of what I was saying. Like one of those out-of-body things. You ever have one of those?"

Dawshinski nodded, though the only out-of-body experiences he had were assisted by 180-proof beverages.

"So I'm talking and not there," Nero said. "I was somewhere else. Somewhere very simple, someplace stripped down to one thought. Or one impulse. And before I was through talking, I was in. You get it? I was in."

"You mean—"

"I mean I knew then that not only did I want it to happen, I knew it would," Nero said. "You ever felt that? It's an urge. But it's more than that. It becomes your entire body. It becomes you. And that's it."

Dawshinski sat there looking at him, waiting for him to remember who he was talking to.

"Right," Nero said. "Right. But drunks don't get indicted."

"At least not just for being drunks," Dawshinski said.

"Sorry."

"Don't worry about it."

Nero took his hands off the table, leaving two sweaty palm prints. He reached over to the curtain and using his index finger parted them about two inches. A crack of sunlight cut across his face.

"Spring's sprung," he said quietly.

"Be the Fourth of July before you know it," Dawshinski offered.

"Fourth of July," Nero said absently. He let the curtain close, blinked and refocused on Dawshinski. "Don't you want to know how long?"

"How long what?"

"How long it went on," Nero said. He didn't wait for an answer. "Five months. Give or take. My office. The car. A couple of motels, including this one. Even a parking lot of a Kentucky Fried Chicken."

"You ever think about—"

"Getting caught? Not really. There was too much stuff going on. Not just with her. Everything was jumbled."

"Jumbled?"

"Lauren, the kids, my real life. They were props in some kind of life I was pretending to have," he said. "The other thing was front and center. It was realer than real. That's the thing. One day I wake up, and what was real and what I'd wished for switched places. You see?"

"I see."

"And you know the next part."

"What's that?"

"The can't-help-yourself part. The can't-get-enough part. You're somewhere and you'd rather be someplace else. You're talking to someone, but you're not really there. It goes from inside your head into the world and when it's let out, it's all over. It's not yours to control anymore."

"You're right," Dawshinski said. "I do know that part."

Nero gave him a quick little smile, then started rubbing his eyes, digging the heels of his palms into his eye sockets and letting out a long, low exhalation.

"When'd you sleep last?" Dawshinski asked.

"Don't know. Day ago. Coupla days."

"When'd you find out?"

"Lawyer got a call from the DA's office."

"That was thoughtful."

"Yeah. Real polite."

"You see it coming?"

"Yeah. Well. I knew something was coming. Something turned."

"You mean her?"

"She changed. Just like that. One minute cold, very distant. The next day all smiles and cuddles. Then back again," Nero said. "She'd lost that thing. You know, that thing I noticed at first. That steadiness. Then she started breaking dates, stopped returning my calls. That's when I knew. It was just a matter of time."

There was another long silence. Nero's palms were back on the table, pressing down. Dawshinski glanced at the TV. Some kind of protest in Europe. Students and workers were squaring off with the police yet again. Dawshinski knew he should ask the question. He'd have to ask it sooner or later. The question. What now? Nero suddenly straightened up and reached behind his back. Dawshinski thought he was stretching, but Nero's right hand came back up to the table and he put it down between them, the heavy clunking noise enough for Dawshinski to know it was real.

"My father's," Nero said.

Dawshinski looked at it, then back up at Nero, who was looking down at the .38. He seemed as surprised as anyone that it had appeared there.

"Got a pearl handle," Nero noted. "Not exactly a family heirloom or anything like that. This is from back in the day when just about every Jersey Italian was carrying."

He spun it as if he were playing spin the bottle. It made a rattling noise on the table top, then stopped with the barrel pointing toward the curtains. Dawshinski was trying to remember if .38s had a safety. He came up blank.

"You remember your algebra?" Nero asked.

"Algebra?"

"Yeah. Algebra. As in math."

"What little I knew I tried hard to forget," Dawshinski said.

"That's a shame," Nero said. "I really liked the story problems. Had 'em in tenth grade, or thereabouts. The other kids hated them. Couldn't figure 'em. The secret was to work them out step by step. Figure out each new factor. Work it through. Go to the next."

He spun the gun again. Dawshinski tried to count the revolutions. It helped distract him. The barrel stopped at the curtains again. He could have asked if it was loaded, but it was a dumb question. This was not a time for dumb questions.

"That's what I've been doing here," Nero said.

Dawshinski looked up from the gun. "Algebra?"

"Story problems," he said. "My story problem. Let x equal this. Let z equal that."

He spun the gun again. The barrel pointed in the opposite direction, toward the beds.

"The thing is that no matter how the story problem lays it out, everything leads to the same place, the same answer," he said. "She's a woman. But she's not. She's learning the language and the angles, step by step. She doesn't know what the next step is until she's there, and then she knows it. You see?"

"I see."

"I don't think you do," Nero said. The fingertips of his right hand were touching the little barrel. "The problem is that you're with her on each step. You're there, and it's exactly where you shouldn't be."

Dawshinski found it hard to look at Nero. He couldn't take his eyes off the gun.

"X equals this. Z equals that. And what does Walter Nero do?"

He spun the gun again. When it stopped it was pointing at Dawshinski. He looked up. Their eyes met. Nero leaned in close, never breaking his stare.

"What I want to know is this: Is there any consideration?"

"Consideration?"

"Is this what it is? They're going to make it what they think it is, and that's what it is," Nero said, leaning so close that Dawshinski could smell the remnants of his egg and sausage breakfast on this breath. "Is there no consideration? None?"

Dawshinski kept looking at him but said nothing. For the first time since he entered the room he was certain about something. He was certain that Nero wasn't expecting an answer to that question. He was working the problem. His story problem. Dawshinski saw it playing across Nero's face, the calculations of a man who's made a mistake. An irretrievable mistake that had cudgeled the trajectory of his life. No more predictability. No more patterns. It came down to this. A motel room off Route 206. Nero leaned back in his chair and let out another long, low breath.

"You know what they'll do, right?" he said. He was looking down into his lap, at his limp hands resting there.

"Sorry?"

"In prison. You know what they'll do. You know what it is, right?"

Dawshinski waited a few moments. "Yes," he finally said. "I know."

Something trilled. A cell phone. Dawshinski had left his in the car. Another trill. Nero broke out of his stillness, straightened his legs under the table, reached into his left jeans pocket, and took out his cell.

"Wife," he said.

It trilled one more time, then stopped.

"I should call her," Nero said weakly.

"You should," Dawshinski said. But it came out too quickly.

Nero almost smiled, then placed the cell on the table, next to the gun.

"I think it's time," he said, "for you to go."

Dawshinski looked at him dumbly for a few seconds.

"It's time for you to go," Nero repeated.

Dawshinski got up slowly, his knees cracking. As he put on his jacket he avoided looking at Nero and glanced at the TV screen. S&P up slightly, Dow tepid. He tried to think of a stalling action, but nothing came. When he was at the door, his hand on the knob, Nero turned in his chair.

"One thing," he said.

"Sure," Dawshinski answered.

"I just want you to say 'Is there anything I can do for you.'"

"Excuse me?"

"I want to hear it. 'Is there anything I can do for you.' Just once. I want to hear it."

Dawshinski stood there with his hand on the knob. He couldn't say the words. They wouldn't come out, held back by a reflexive embarrassment that he already knew he'd be ashamed of.

"Forget it," Nero said, turning away from Dawshinski. He spun the gun. Dawshinski didn't look to see where it pointed. "Dash?"

"Yes?"

"You know, you're in for a world of shit," Nero said, not turning to face him. "For coming here. I know that. I want you to know I know that."

"I know you do," Dawshinski said.

"I'm saying I appreciate it," Nero said. "Okay?"

"Don't worry about it," Dawshinski said.

Nero didn't say anything. He didn't turn. Dawshinski took one more look into the gloom of the room, the quivering light of the TV edging back the shadows then melting into them.

"Wally?"

Nero didn't turn.

"Wally?"

Nero twisted his chair to face him. Their eyes met.

"Is there anything I can do for you?"

Nero looked at him for a few moments, then turned back to the table. Dawshinski stepped out of the room and closed the door as quietly as he could, blinking in the warm light. Spring had sprung. When he reached the stairs and started walking down, he waited for the sound. With each step he waited and on the eighth step he heard it, surprisingly quiet, almost delicate, a moist popping sound heard just above the soft whine of tires on the turnpike.

FREDDY

Julie Dearborn

The day Freddy died I was at a conference for English teachers. When not in a session, I sat in front of the enormous fireplace in the lodge and re-read *Safekeeping*, my favorite memoir. It was sitting on a shelf in the classroom and I borrowed it for the afternoon. It is a story of loss and coming to terms with one's choices. To this day I connect Freddy's death, his unhappy life, and our estrangement to this book.

I had been bracing myself for the news I was about to get ever since Freddy was fired from the first job he'd had in 30 years. He'd finally applied for disability after my mother insisted. Before the government would give him disability, they made him take a job to prove he couldn't hold one. I don't know if I really thought getting fired from Walmart would make him suicidal, but I knew something was going to happen to him and I knew it wasn't going to be good. He was forced, once again, to come face to face with his life choices. Once again, he was rejected by the world he'd tried so hard to hide from. My mother was with him when he collapsed in the family room. She and my sister Liz were with him when he died. Greg, my youngest brother, listened on speakerphone when they took him off whatever machine was keeping him alive in the hospital. I was thousands of miles away, walking on the beach. Wanting a weekend free of distractions, I'd left the phone in my purse uncharged; I came home Sunday afternoon to a voice mailbox clogged with messages.

Greg's message was simple: call me right away.

"Did he kill himself?" I asked when he told me our brother was dead.

"No, he had a stroke."

We made plans to fly from San Francisco to Kansas City the next day. I called my boss at work and arranged a week of lesson plans for the substitute teacher, threw some things in a bag, and took a Xanax.

When he was very young and learning new words every day, Freddy gazed out the window of the car on long drives and at regular intervals announced, "mailbox, mailbox, mailbox," pointing to each one the car passed. We all laughed, but it didn't seem truly funny to me. I didn't know the word *irony* then, but I felt it each time Freddy said mailbox. Our father delivered mail for a living, and even then I knew that he was not the kind of man who should raise a child like Freddy. Dad, also named Frederick, was as temperamentally different from his namesake as a Bengal Tiger is from a kitten. Dad was a bitter survivor of a childhood scarred by a shiftless alcoholic father, and anger drove him. The other three of us managed to survive his verbal abuse and his unpredictable expressions of rage, but Freddy was fragile and less able to cope. Back in the 1970s no one knew about Asperger's syndrome, the mild form of autism that I am sure he had. I learned about it when I read a *New York Times* article in the '80s and recognized my brother; he was in his twenties then and his life already seemed to be going nowhere. His difficulty adapting to social norms made him surly and fearful. The drip drip drip of Dad's verbal abuse crushed him.

I started worrying about him when I was 12. That day everybody was outside on the asphalt playground that bled into the parking lot of St. Patrick's elementary school, waiting to be picked up after school. Mom was waiting in the blue Chevy for me, my sister Liz, and Freddy. I had on the gray and green plaid skirt and white blouse that I wore every day. As I walked past the steps at the end of the playground, my classmate Dennis came up to me and said, "Your brother is in a fight." I turned and saw a pile of boys, my brother in there somewhere. I kept walking to the car. No part of me wanted to try to break up or join the fight. The best thing to do, I knew, was to tell Mom. So that's what I did. She somehow got him out of the fight. All she had to do was stand over the boys and say, "What's going on here?" and they dispersed. Kids at St. Patrick's respected adults—or at least pretended to.

It was not that unusual for a nine-year-old boy to get in a fight. Freddy had a few scrapes and bruises; he bruised easily and he bled more than the rest of us, but the physical wounds from this fight were soon gone. What makes this memory significant is that it's the moment I realized my brother was going to add another layer of trauma to my life. In addition to my chronically angry, verbally abusive father, the constant fights between him and my mother, the intense sibling rivalry between my sister and me, Freddy was going to be a problem. I looked at him sitting in the front seat next to my mother and I saw it all: He was going to keep getting into trouble, he would never fit in, he would always be misunderstood and different, his life would always cast a shadow over mine. And that's what happened.

He was a gentle person who scared people. He could read books before he started kindergarten, but he couldn't read facial expressions. He grew into an adult whose isolation and fear of the world made him appear suspicious. He seemed rude when he was really just scared of the rejection he constantly got. He was kicked out of a library because the librarian didn't like his expression. A policeman beat him up because he didn't like the tone of his voice. He was unlucky. He was passive. He had the soul of a poet and the personality of a long-winded university professor. He could talk for hours about American history and by the first grade knew the name of every US president and his running mate in chronological order. While touring the White House during a family vacation in Washington, DC, when he was about seven, he pointed to a painting and said, in a tone usually used when spotting a celebrity, "Look! It's Millard Fillmore!"

In many photographs he has a serious, almost glum expression, but in photographs with animals he beams. When our cat Petunia had kittens, he wrote a journal of the final days of her pregnancy. It ended with the sentence, "Cougar is born." Cougar was the kitten we got to keep and Freddy got to name him. Cougar lived for only a few years before drowning in a neighbor's pool. Freddy was inconsolable.

After he got suspended from the public middle school for smoking pot in the cloakroom, my parents made one of their many attempts to help him. Thinking, probably correctly, that a public school was not the right environment for someone with his temperament, they sent him to a Catholic boarding school called Savior of the World. They hoped a more controlled environment would keep him out of trouble. The secret hope of all of us was that the school would live up to its name and save him. It didn't, but it did shelter him for a while. He didn't get into any trouble there, though I found out later that there was just as much marijuana at Savior of the World as at any other high school in the late 1970s. We all went to his graduation. Watching him cross the stage in a cap and gown to receive his diploma, I felt hopeful that he would find his place in the world.

Freddy had his first major breakdown in college. He made it public during an algebra test. The stress of trying to solve some equation or decipher one of those indecipherable word problems must have brought all of his pain and despair to a head. He walked up to the professor, held out his blank test, and muttered something like "I can't take it anymore." This got the attention of the professor and my parents. The school recommended that he take an incomplete in the class and a break from school. My parents did their best to help him. They found some sort of Catholic group home for people with emotional problems. Mom took Greg, Liz, and me to visit him over Christmas break. The three of us sat there in the visiting room listening to him talk about all the strange characters staying there and I fought back tears. I hadn't wanted to go. I loved Freddy, but I was tired of watching him flounder and devolve. I wanted to live my life without constantly being reminded of my childhood.

The group home didn't help him in any meaningful way, but it got him through his senior year. He graduated from college and moved back into my parents' house where he stayed for the rest of his life. Graduating from college was the beginning of my liberation and I wanted Freddy to be liberated too, but within a month of graduating he got into the worst trouble of his life. It was June and he'd gone to have a beer with some guys from the neighborhood. They were standing outside a 7-11 drinking the watered-down Coors beer that was legal in Kansas for anyone over 18. A cop pulled up, probably looking for an excuse to start something. Mom found out later that he had already unlawfully killed at least two people in the line of duty and gotten away with it. How it began I don't know. I just know how it ended. The cop must not have liked the way Freddy talked to him or looked at him. He entered his name in the system and saw that there was a bench warrant out for Frederick Dearborn. Dad had been cited a few years earlier for having his dog off leash and never paid the fine. In most instances my father was scrupulously law abiding, but in this case the law was up against his cheapness and his cheapness won. He probably saw it as a form of civil disobedience not to pay the fine. Once the cop saw the name come up on the computer he asked no questions, just threw Freddy to the pavement hard enough to draw blood, punched him in the face a couple of times, handcuffed him, and took him to jail for something that he didn't do.

I was just beginning to build my own life. I'd moved to San Francisco and was feeling free of all the painful drama, but it was all still happening thousands of miles away. After his experience with violent injustice, Freddy stopped trying. He started paying less attention to his appearance; eventually his hair became disheveled and he wore dingy frayed T-shirts; his expression was furtive, he didn't make eye contact. It was as if he wanted people to fear and shun him. I never feared him, but I resented him. I didn't exactly shun him, but I kept as much distance as I could between us. He didn't make sense to me. Why couldn't he find a way to fit in? I had the same father and I'd managed to do it. Why couldn't he?

Freddy was gentle, sensitive, and gifted. He was also the most enormous pain in the ass I have ever known. The year he was thrown in jail, Mom paid for him to visit me in San Francisco for two weeks. He was still clinging to normalcy, his grooming hadn't deteriorated yet, and he was young enough that we all still held out hope for him. Maybe this visit would inspire him to take action instead of hiding in his bedroom reading and listening to music. He came with two bags, one a yellow backpack full of books that sat next to him whenever he was in my apartment. During the day while I was at work, he wandered the city, went to used bookstores, and sat in cafés, using the spending money Mom gave him to buy coffee and books. One day he ran all the way from my apartment in the Castro to Ocean Beach. I took him to movies and a concert. When I wasn't with him, I worried, knowing his gift for getting into trouble, and was relieved every evening when I came home from work and he was safely in my apartment, reading.

The second week of the visit, I escorted him to visit relatives across the bay. He stayed with them for four days, hanging out with our cousin Jack, and when it was time for him to come back to the city, the day before his flight back home, he refused. The plan was for him to get on BART at three so he'd be downtown before it got dark and then follow the bus route I'd written down for him to my apartment. I called at three o'clock; he hadn't left.

"When are you leaving?"

"Don't worry. I'll leave soon."

At four o'clock he hadn't left.

"Don't get your panties in a bundle," he said. "I'll get there."

At six o'clock, he still wasn't back. The thought of him alone at night, taking public transportation in an unfamiliar part of the city, with zero social skills, alarmed me. I called again.

"Yeah, yeah, yeah, stop worrying, I'll get there."

"Let me talk to Jack."

Jack came to the phone and I said, "You need to make him leave. He doesn't know San Francisco. I don't want him downtown when it's dark."

There was always a selfishness about Freddy. He was having a good time with Jack, feeling safe and relaxed and accepted, and he didn't want the feeling to end. He didn't think or care how his actions affected me, or anyone else. Perhaps he was incapable. My entire evening was spent imagining worst-case scenarios. I was exhausted at work the next day.

"It's kind of weird in San Francisco at night," he said when he walked into my apartment at ten o'clock, "but I wasn't scared."

I remembered my own experiences waiting for a bus at night when I first moved to San Francisco, and I knew my brother well enough to know when he was lying. You were freaked out, I thought, and you got what you deserved.

He fell in love with San Francisco, just as I had, and he wanted to come back. On a more permanent basis. He didn't have the courage to ask me himself, so he got Mom to do it.

"Do you think Freddy could come and stay with you for a while? I'll pay his expenses of course."

Hell no, I thought. Where exactly would he stay? I had a roommate. There were only two bedrooms in my apartment. Only one bathroom. What would my landlord think? I had a job and a life. My life. Not my family's. Mine. I'd worked hard to create it and it wasn't fair of Mom to ask this of me. Why was she putting me in a position to reject Freddy? It hurt to do it, but I did reject him. He called me a few weeks after I told Mom he wouldn't be moving in with me. "San

Francisco is okay, but I wouldn't like living there, it's too crowded," he said.

I rarely saw or spoke to him after that. I sent birthday cards and Christmas presents, but he never responded. He eventually descended into paranoia and could talk about nothing but how corrupt America was. It didn't matter who was president, Freddy hated him and considered the entire government evil.

When Freddy was in his forties, Dad got Alzheimer's and Freddy became his caretaker: he gave him baths, changed his diapers, dressed and undressed him, cooked for him and fed him when he couldn't feed himself. Mom couldn't have managed without him and we were all grateful. When Dad finally died, we were all there for the funeral. All except Freddy. "I don't like to go to things like that," he said. We wanted him to know we appreciated what he'd done, so we bought him a card mocking George W. Bush—Obama was president then, but Bush was still his favorite president to hate. Five years later, he died.

I was not there the day my brother collapsed, not there when they drilled a hole in the side of his head in an attempt to save him. I was not there when they unplugged him. I was not there when Mom stroked his face and said, "my son, my son." I was not there when my sister said, "Mom, I think he's passed."

I'm glad I was unreachable. I'd carpooled to the conference and had no way of getting back to San Francisco until the next day—even if I had known what was happening I would have been trapped there. Not all the Xanax in the world could have kept me from crawling out of my skin.

The hour he died I was at the beach. I saw four deer walking on the dunes. One of them had enormous antlers and I thought how heavy they looked. All four walked together for a bit, and then the one with the antlers sank to its knees and stayed perfectly still. I watched for a few minutes as the other three kept walking down the beach, toward the horizon.

I Told You Not to Move

Allison Flom

I was standing at the top of the ladder leading to the twisty slide and I could see the wrinkles on the top of your head while you talked to Carmen's dad about golf and I jumped and I didn't think it would hurt you I just wanted to see if I could fly. I couldn't. You crashed into the pavement and your face was all bruised and bloody when they put you in an ambulance and when you got home from the hospital you said Come on Mary that was something only an idiot would do, are you crazy, are you fucking crazy? You're too big, far too fat to jump on top of another person's head. And when you were walking up the stairs to your room you muttered something like Jesus Christ, I mean, a fucking 12-year-old? Why were we even at the fucking playground? Ow, dammit, fuck.

Beard Face's girlfriend comes in with a peach pie like she does every Tuesday except this time her hair is way shorter. She walks in saying sooooo like her voice is the drumroll for an important announcement like who's the next president or winner of a singing show. Oh, no. Beard Face says Oh, Natalia, it's terrible. Oh man, did you—ugh, yeah, it's not good. She cries and then closes the curtain while she says something like she wishes she could do everything right to make him happy and how could she change it to make it prettier for him. We keep the curtains open usually. There's a crack in the wall on his side of the room that faces into another room where we can sometimes see people having sex. And my side of the room has the good clock, plus the fridge so we can both see what they're putting in there for the next day. We always know what lunch will be. We're like detectives.

Beard Face and I aren't friends. I won't even give him the courtesy of a proper name in here, but I like him better than the other roommates I've had so my mom signed a thing saying she's fine with her daughter sharing a room with a man. Beard Face is mean to his girlfriend and has cool tattoos and usually thinks it's 1971 and we just saw John Lennon at the Filmore East and I never correct him because I would have loved to do that if I was in New York / alive in 1971. It's more entertaining to play along. He says I'm the only woman in the world who's not annoying and I like how he says I'm a woman because everyone else seems sure I'm not one yet and I'm not quite free to decide.

There are two pictures on the wall in 210B, both of fruit bowls. When we get fruit here it's usually in one of those little plastic containers with the lid that's fun to pull off. The only other thing that Beard Face and I have in common is that we like to save those plastic containers and put them in a shoebox in the closet. We're halfway convinced we'll need them one day but mostly it's funny how a nurse will find it every once in a while. She'll open it, say her own bedside manner version of What the fuck are these lunatics thinking and if I report it no one will take me seriously because who really gives a flying fuck if these sad losers collect plastic containers from mandarin oranges? So they throw out the containers and we start over but no one's ever tried to stop us or say anything. One time we got to 91 and a half containers before they were discovered, that's the record. (The half is because I counted 91 and Beard Face counted 92 and we didn't have time for a recount.)

I always left a spoon in the butter section of the refrigerator door. I know you said I couldn't eat dessert, but we always had cake in there, so whenever you left the room I could hide in the refrigerator for a few quick bites with my auxiliary spoon. And I know you wanted us to look like your boss's kids in their Christmas card because they looked classic. And then you didn't want to do the photos when November came around because we didn't look classic enough and Mom is even prettier than your boss's wife and you and him are both almost bald, wrinkly, and grumpy so I knew it was my fault when you said that everyone was responsible for the inconvenience.

I don't like anything about the word fat. I think it makes people look fat when they say it. It's ugly and it's supposed to describe something ugly. And I know I was. Fat, I mean. But you told Mom Maybe we wouldn't have wasted money on a photographer if you had more control of what she ate and You cook with so much oil and All the guys would laugh at me if they saw the picture, can you imagine? Merry Christmas from us and our daughter who can't beat obesity and you know, warm wishes! JoAnn we're the only couple who doesn't bring our kid to the holiday party, you know that? And she said Quiet Frank she might hear you and you said If she could just lose the weight and some other stuff but we went to the park anyway without the photographer and I think that was the day we saw two pigeons fighting.

They usually do Beard Face's sessions in 210B, which means I have to leave for two hours, which is okay. I usually go to the end of the hall and play Connect Four with the retards. I don't like that word either because I think people look retarded when they say it but I can't change it, that's what they are. Bony Fingers always wins because she plays alone all day and she knows all the tricks. Sometimes she asks if she can read me her poetry and I almost always say yes even though poems are just a bunch of words put together and I think anyone can write one.

I come back into 210B and Beard Face is crying after his session and I don't ask why because that's the wrong thing to do. Some days you go to sleep and you're like, this was a great day, you know? I nod. He's weird. And if you're in like a group of people or fuckin' uh, you know, whatever, you should want everyone to have that feeling like as much as possible, right? He has an octopus tattooed on his forearm and once he told me he can't see it because we can't have mirrors here but it's right there on his forearm. I don't feel that way about anyone in this place. I don't give a fuck if they have a good day. I tell him I don't either and he tells me I'm stupid then he gets in the shower.

Gus (my favorite janitor) comes in to change the trash bags and he shakes one of them out and there's some sticky liquid on it and it gets all over me and I scream. He's really scared. A nurse comes running in as though he was trying to murder me, which is racist because he is black. He is the best person who works here. And then I don't remember but I think I have a tantrum and I'm sticky and I can't stand it on my elbows and they take me to another room to shower immediately because Beard Face is in our shower still because he's an asshole.

And since it's not my shower the mean nurse (Pointy Boob) has to help me and I don't like how she's putting the soap on a loofa because I don't know whose loofa it is so I scream a lot, more than usual. So Bony Fingers comes in (I guess it's her room but I'm not sure and it's not important) and she starts reading a stupid poem about how snow is God's punishment for sinners and she stands there like an idiot watching me shower.

It snowed like four feet one weekend during sixth grade and you told me to put on those big boots that are like ten pounds each and go into the snow with you. Mom did that little jump she does when she hears an idea that's good in theory but she knows she doesn't have to participate and she started making hot chocolate right away. You told her to make it with water instead of milk and really half the packet is more than enough. I said I didn't want any but I did.

We had to take huge steps to trudge through the snow and it took like a half hour to get to the end of our driveway and you asked me Can you imagine the calories we're burning? This is like hiking! And then I felt like going back inside but I stayed out with you and we made a giant snowball and pushed it up the hill while you yelled Muscle, muscle, muscle!

It's snowing now and all the nurses are talking about it. Dr. Kaplan comes in with his usual Heeeey there because he's passive and a little scared of us and an idiot. He asks how I'm feeling this morning and I ask him if he has any kids to play with in the snow and he tells me I've already asked that before. Two daughters, dumbass, Beard Face chimes in and then he apologizes for calling me a dumbass and tells me he loves me. Dr. Kaplan closes the curtain.

I don't love anyone. It seems exhausting and pointless and when you don't love anyone it's easier to die. We have a radio in here and on Thursday nights there's a radio show called Lloyd Loves Love (sometimes I ask Beard Face to say it three times fast and he looks like an idiot). Lloyd interviews couples that are happy. That's the whole premise. They talk about how they met and cute little anecdotes that have the women saying I swear I looked my worst that day and the men saying I had never seen anyone look more beautiful and then she giggles like Awww, Timothy and Lloyd is like Isn't thaaaat sweet. And we can't even see what they look like so there's no way for us to have our own opinions, we just have to listen. They don't have gay couples on the show that much but one time there were these two women who met in the cereal aisle of a grocery store and Beard Face asked me if I think Natalia is gay and if I like cereal.

I said no to both questions because I didn't want their relationship to end and granola makes me shit a lot in the good way. I like when she's here. I feel bad when he's mean to her but it reminds me how not mean he is to me usually and how shitty it would be to love someone.

All the other kids are gonna be in bathing suits and I'm just looking out for you, kiddo. I didn't mention that I could just wear a T-shirt over my one-piece because I liked that you were trying to convince me not to go on the school trip. Carmen texted me pictures from the hotel that literally every sophomore except me was staying at and all the captions were like Feel better, we miss you because I had to say I was sick because I obviously couldn't say it was because I was too fat for the trip, that wouldn't even make sense. Mom was right, I could have gone, I might have liked it even. But you wanted me to stay home and so I did.

That was the day we went to the farmers market. You didn't let me eat anything because it was between lunch and dinner but we walked around and talked to all the vendors and the flower guy with the red beard offered me a summer job. I felt like I was being more productive than all those other idiots on the school trip because I was networking while they went in a stupid grimy hotel pool.

Ethan comes in for the first time at 3:34 a.m. on Wednesday. I have an alarm set for every time all the numbers are the same so I can make a wish. The alarm was going off at 3:33 and I was making a really long and complicated wish so it took the full minute, which is definitely allowed, and I thought I was dreaming when I saw him opening the refrigerator. It's dark and quiet like it is during 1:11 a.m., 2:22 a.m., 3:33 a.m., and 4:44 a.m. There are always nurses and janitors shuffling around by 5:55 a.m. so those are the most special ones because I can focus entirely on my wishes and no one else knows I'm awake. Beard Face doesn't mind the alarms and almost always sleeps through them but if he wakes up we make eye contact and don't say anything because we're both focusing on our own wishes and acknowledging that each other are awake but in deep focus.

I see Ethan's disproportionate shadow on the wall behind him, composed entirely by darkness and the light struggling through cracks in the bathroom door. He's not more than four feet tall with skinny legs and a chunky blue helmet on his head. He pushes the handle in and releases it like he's opened this fridge a million times. There are eight miniature cartons of orange juice on the middle shelf. He opens each one with the same movement, exaggerated in his elbow and steady in his hands, and pours it onto the ground just inches in front of his bare feet.

At first I'm thinking what the fuck but I'm not scared. I fight my eyelids to stay awake, since I'm so used to falling asleep after every wish knowing I have only an hour and eleven minutes of uninterrupted sleep before the next one. And I'm wondering if I'm dreaming but I don't think my subconscious imagination could create him. After the eighth carton is emptied out and placed on the bottom shelf his hands sweep the middle shelf once more. He closes the fridge with care and steps just past the light and towards the door.

Aunt Kate got drunk at my sixteenth birthday dinner and asked you about the day I was born. You suggested that Mom's water broke on your new car seats. She scrunched up her face and swatted her hand in front of it like she does when she wants the subject to change and then you cut right to the hospital room. You said the doctor who delivered me positioned me in Mom's arms so my face was facing you directly. And then something about I knew she was pregnant, oh believe me I knew, I just didn't expect there to be a baby at the end of it and then you said I had never seen anything so beautiful.

And well I'm just wondering if that means you thought I was beautiful or if you were speaking more about the miracle of life in general because I've never known you to talk about things generally. And if you were talking about me I just wonder like if that was the only time you thought that about me. Or if you ever thought it again you know, after that time.

I feel his 3:34 presence before I see his toes on the linoleum inching toward the sliver of light. He stands in it fully for only a second before he becomes a shadow (over the wall with one of the fruit bowl pictures) opening the refrigerator. He leaves the door to 210B closed this time and it's supposed to be halfway open into the hallway. He starts with a carton on the left and begins the identical routine. I listen more to the sound of the juice hitting the floor this time. It sounds messy in a safe way. I try not to imagine how sticky it will be.

Next, the door is thrown open and four people run into our room. They turn on the lights, which Beard Face is not happy about. It's loud. It's two nurses, a security guard, and maybe even a doctor. I've never seen him before but he has a V-neck and chest hair so I assume he's a doctor. I don't think there's any need for doctors to wear V-necks and I don't think there's any need for what most of the doctors in this building do. They scream.

Ethan! No! NO! Stop that, now, Ethan, stop it immediately. Nurse #1 smacks a carton out of his hands mid-pour and shakes him by his shoulders. He musters a faint moan and his voice sounds like a baby's. What is all this? Very bad, Ethan. Bad behavior. The security guard picks him up with no regard for his left arm, which is folded violently between the guard's chest and the rest of his body. Nurse #2 mutters Ugh, Christ and cleans up the juice.

Sorry for the commotion, guys. Go back to sleep, all right? Beard Face offers a half-conscious Turn the fucking light off and she does, as she leaves, the ground free from juice and his presence erased. I'm still awake when my 4:44 goes off.

You took me to that costume store that had all my favorite characters. It didn't take me that long to figure out that none of the costumes would fit me but it was nice that you really still wanted me to like Halloween; you just didn't let us have candy in the house. But that was the same year Mom felt bad about turning away trick-or-treaters again so she put a bowl of candy by the front door and you were really, really mad. But it's because you were looking out for me and thinking maybe I'd fit into one of those costumes the next year.

I loved all the magical characters. The princesses who could fight dragons were just as cool as the dragons themselves and the jesters and the serpents and I would have dressed up as any of it. Carmen wanted us to dress up as the princesses but I didn't want to commit to that because I was going to the costume store with you and maybe I would find something even cooler. She dressed up as the princesses with Amanda. Nothing at the costume store fit me, not even the knight costume for boys. You bought me a crown and long gloves and a sword and Mom made me that cape dress. I don't think she stitched it very well because it ripped down the middle and I didn't even eat candy that night, honest. I spent all my wishes that month on suddenly developing allergies to candy and then I didn't want to test it that day in case they came true.

I'm worried that I didn't think hard enough about my 3:33 wish. I know it kind of danced in and out of my mind but I don't think I focused enough and I'm scared the universe will think I'm not dedicated to it so I have to expand a little and do the unthinkable: both 12:34s, and maybe even the 1:23s, 2:34s, 3:45s, and 4:56s.

He carries his body just the same, unaffected by the trouble of the previous night. He leads with his toes and tiny knees and he kind of glides, like if you could only see the top of his body you might think he was rollerblading. He pauses, his upper body in the light and his eyes gray and empty when he looks at me. I whisper hello and he says hi like a reflex barely moving his mouth. He faces me for another moment and then proceeds to the refrigerator.

He's pouring out the third carton when Nurse #2, the security guard, and another nurse come in. The guard pulls him by the arm away from the fridge so hard that it could have popped out of the socket and he screams. He throws himself onto the floor and he's yelling indistinguishable words. He smacks his palms on the linoleum and writhes in pain. The new nurse tries to pick him up but he kicks her in the face. He doesn't mean to hurt her. He's just swinging his tiny feet where her face is and then the security guard puts plastic binds on his hands, like handcuffs mixed with those zip tie things they use to hang the parking lot signs for the middle school carnival.

Not okay, Ethan! Very bad! They're talking over his screaming and Beard Face is not happy about the disturbance. When the commotion ends we're both awake and Beard Face starts talking about a girl he met when he was backpacking (what a silly word for a silly activity) and I listen until the morning.

The next afternoon Nurse #1, Nurse #2, and the New Nurse come in with a middle-aged couple. I know they aren't Beard Face's parents because they don't have any tattoos and if Beard Face even had parents he wouldn't be all fucked up but I think they must be friends of his because people never come in here. I imagine what it would be like if my mom came to visit. She'd hate it here—the tiled floors, the pictures of the fruit bowls, the amount of female doctors (she doesn't trust women)—but she wouldn't try to get me out or anything. She'd complain and maybe bring some hot cocoa.

But it's better that she doesn't. She always sends postcards from wherever she's traveling. Her friend had told her to start fresh and travel and something about she deserves to have some fun after all this. Last month I put one of her postcards from Europe on the wall of 210B as Beard Face sang Mary's mom loves Madrid more than she loves Mary. I didn't mind. The song was catchy and the content was true and Beard Face loves when the consonants in a sentence match and make poetry like that.

The nurses and the middle-aged couple are muttering quietly until Nurse #1 can see that I'm looking at them and writing things down, which makes her nervous and I think it's funny when people who work here feel threatened by a pencil and paper. And, this is the refrigerator for the whole floor. We keep food in room number 10 on all the floors, so he may have known where it is, but obviously he came down four flights of stairs to get here. The woman asks how long it took and the nurse tells her We can't be sure how long he was in here before we arrived, but he had spilled a lot of juice onto the floor, which is of course a hazard. The woman offers an absent Of course, of course and puts her hand to her head.

I can't believe this, John. There's just no answer, like it isn't, I can't—oh, God. John (I guess) comforts her. They study the path to the refrigerator like a crime scene. How could—I just don't see—

Then the Scary Alarm goes off. There are three alarms, all of them on the same system but they all make slightly different sounds and I know this one is the scariest. It's only happened twice since I've been here. Gus says it means someone is dying but janitors aren't supposed to tell us things. When it goes off, everyone in that unit (not us obviously) has to go right to the nurse's station. I'm so sorry, you'll have to excuse me for just a moment, Mr. and Mrs. Thompson. Nurse #1 leaves the woman and John in my room. Beard Face is sleeping and I can tell he's being an idiot in his dreams.

I say hi. I tell them he wasn't in here for more than a minute. I tell them the staff was violent and Ethan didn't mean any harm I just know it. I tell them I didn't mind the orange juice on the ground, he did it the night before too and no one knew. They didn't come get him? How did he get back to his room? I tell them I'm not sure, I just cleaned up the orange juice with paper towels after he left and didn't see him again until the next night, which was two nights ago, and I didn't mind the disturbance. I'm awake at that time anyway, I tell them.

You don't sleep? John's voice is deep and gravelly and he has a moustache that takes up most of his face. I don't want to tell them about the wishes so I say I never sleep And how long have you been here? How much longer do you have to stay? They laugh when I say probably forever so I laugh too and they change the subject.

Well, we thought Ethan would be out by now. Can I ask what you're writing? I explain that this week I'm supposed to write things that I want to tell you and include seven memories I have of you and I don't think Dr. Kaplan really reads it so I'm doing only sort of what he says because I only sort of care what he thinks about me. They nod at the comfort of doctors' orders and offer, He was switched around a lot before they put him in Epilepsy (capitalized because it's the name of the unit on the sixth floor but he also has it, I guess) but he was never on this floor. So the juice thing is all the more shocking, just befuddling, really. We'll have him come down and apologize to you, for the mess and disturbance and all. We're sorry, we don't understand it, it's—and she puts her hand to her head again. I tell them he has nothing to be sorry about, honest.

In the car on our way to my first day of Jenny Craig you reminded me twice to tell them that my goal was to lose the weight to fit in a prom dress, and prom was only eight months away. I didn't tell them that. I was the youngest one there by at least 20 years and each person had to say everything we eat in an average day and then the woman sitting next to the scale would comment on it and say what we were doing wrong.

She furrowed her eyebrows as soon as I started talking but I think it was because she felt bad for me. I didn't fit in, like the program director told us when we signed up. I had braces and sneakers and it was Saturday morning and everyone else my age was in SAT prep. The first thing she said was I should only eat the amount of a banana that measures from the tip of my pinky to the base of my palm and any more than that was too much sugar, more than your body will know what to do with. It can't metabolize so it gets stored as fat. Takeaway from the first day: bananas are why I'm fat.

You picked me up at noon with a chopped salad in the backseat and made me thank you for bringing a snack. I told you that bananas were making me fat and I told you about the finger measurement thing and as soon as we got home you told Mom to throw out all the bananas and she did. Just looking out for you, kiddo. You flipped the pages of the newspaper while I buried my face in one of the purple pillows on the couch and screamed as loud as I could, which still felt pretty quiet. Let it out, it's all part of the process.

John and Marcia tell me about Ethan's childhood. Ethan's in an MRI and John says he'll explode if he has to smell the cafeteria again so they're sitting in my room. They tell me that Ethan likes writing and ice cream (I tell them I do too, both things) and he has to wear a helmet because he throws himself on the floor when he's having a tantrum and they don't know what's wrong with him but they're exhausted and they're lucky they get good insurance from Marcia's job and all they want is for him to get better.

I tell them I'm not going to get better. Marcia starts to offer Hey, don't say that—but John nudges her in what someone with a moustache would think is a subtle way and she realizes she knows better than to tell a lunatic that one day they won't be the only thing that they are, which is a lunatic. Then they say they're sorry and I tell them I don't use that word. There's nothing I hate more than apologies. And the beach. The two things I hate the most are the beach and saying sorry.

I ask them if maybe tonight the nurses can just let him spill out all the juices and let it take its course. Let me clean up the juice. He'll spill it all out and walk back to his room, I know it. John tells me that's an insane idea and I make him feel bad about the word choice and I promise that I'll call a nurse immediately if something is wrong. I tell them that since it's not a common thing for people to enjoy spilling orange juice on the floor he probably feels like he's the first guy to ever do it and that's probably overwhelming and ultimately how could he not do it, just to see?

Ethan's late this time: 3:45, he walks in right during my new wish slot but I have a feeling the universe won't mind. The beam of light from the bathroom cuts across his face in a triangle that illuminates only his eyes and right cheek before he reaches the refrigerator door and proceeds peacefully. When the damage is done, he turns to go and his body begins to shake. Not in the scary way (sometimes Beard Face shakes in the scary way and one of the alarms goes off so I can confirm that this was not a scary shake), he just clutches the rail on the side of my bed until it passes and he's fully conscious. Are the nurses coming? His voice is like violins and his breaths are shallow like his lungs are in his shoulders.

I tell him no, only if he needs them, and he shakes his head no rapidly within the massive helmet. He examines the juice around his feet. I made a mess. I tell him don't worry, I'm happy to clean it up, I don't even like juice so he did us both a favor. Oh no, it's all over. I'm sorry. This is your room right? I'm sorry, I'm sorry. I tell him don't say sorry. I don't mind and no one else has to know.

His whisper is tiny but powerful like his arms. His body looks like he's turning to leave but his hands grip my bedrail and the helmet overwhelms his face. I tell him to stop apologizing and my tone is harsher than I intend. I tell him we should never say sorry. When you can say sorry so easily it means you're a person who says sorry a lot, and people who say sorry a lot must fuck up a lot and why do you want to be around someone like that?

But when you do something bad and you say sorry, you take it back. I estimate that he's 12. And then you're free. I start to say something but I get a kind of itchy dry feeling in my throat like the words are tying themselves to my esophagus and getting all mixed up so I just watch him grip the bedrail and shuffle his feet.

So did I wake you up? No. I tell him about the wishes. I thought it would do him some good and he loves it, he shrieks in delight and I clutch his wrist to keep his volume at a whisper and I know we're not supposed to touch anyone but there are a lot of rules and a lot of exceptions to those rules. Do you want me to wish for you to get better?

No. I tell him I already am better, but it's complicated and I'll probably never get out of here so he shouldn't waste his wishes on me. Are you going to die here? I say yeah maybe. He scratches the exterior of his helmet as though it's his head. His gray eyes dart from me to the puddle of juice. He says Maybe me too and he thanks me and he goes back to his room and I change all the rest of my wishes to keeping Ethan alive long enough to leave this place and feel the wind on his skin and spill juice wherever he pleases.

If I asked a hundred people whether they'd rather be fat or crazy I think they'd say crazy and if I asked whether they'd rather be fat or be a criminal I think they'd get stressed out because maybe it's not an obvious answer. We were on the roof, taking down Christmas lights in the second week of February. You told me People only really judge you if you still have Christmas decorations up on Valentine's Day, and any time before then is acceptable. I giggled.

The sun was bouncing off the snow just enough to make me squint when I looked down in your direction. I was above you, gripping the chimney and holding one end of the string of lights. You balanced on the lower part of the roof, gathering the other end. You asked if any of my friends had dates for Valentine's Day and I told you I didn't know and you said Maybe they didn't tell you because they feel bad. I don't know, I always had dates for Valentine's Day, but maybe kids aren't doing it these days and then Well wait until they see you in your prom dress, that'll show 'em. You're gonna be so—ugh, it'll be great, kiddo.

The program that morning was about safe fruits and vegetables, the ones that will burn fat and metabolize quickly and celery is the only food that actually burns calories because it contains no calories but it burns calories to consume and all I can see is celery and you and the prom dress that maybe won't come from a plus-size store two towns away if I dedicate all of my Saturdays from now until then to losing the weight as you always called it and I was never sure which part of me the weight really referred to and what it would be like when that part was gone. I was standing on the highest point of the roof under the naked sky and I felt like I could see everything, when really I could just see the end of our empty street, and our mailbox, and the wrinkles on the top of your head. My shirt was riding up inside my jacket and I wanted to go inside since it had already been a long day and I was hungry but I knew we had a lot more lights to take down. I asked you if we could take a break and you didn't say anything, I think you were muttering to yourself about Valentine's Day while you dismantled another row of lights and the bundle in your hands was getting bigger and more unmanageable. I took a careful step down toward you to repeat my question and I slipped a little. My left knee folded under and I slid just a few inches down toward you before catching my fall with both hands forward.

Oh! Fuck! Come on Mary. I told you not to move from up there. I told you I just wanted to go inside and I didn't know if you could hear me. The wind was in my hair and it felt so clean, like no one else had touched that specific wind before, like I was the first person to ever stand on a roof and feel it. Almost gave me a heart attack, God, are you crazy? Are you fucking crazy?

I know you're gone and you can't read this, which is why Dr. Kaplan's activity is stupid and he's an idiot and I know I'll probably never read this again and no one probably ever will because I'm not going to get famous from this bed but this is the seventh entry and I'm done with this assignment so I'll say the thing I hate to say the most because I almost mean it and I think I will mean it someday and maybe then I'll be free. I'm sorry, Daddy. I didn't mean to push you. I just wanted to see if you could fly.

JAY

Will Schick

Our classes always start with a video clip. An MQ-1 Reaper hovers over an area, and surveils a group of military-aged males (MAMs). We listen to the pilot talk. He's cleared to engage. A hellfire missile darts across the screen in milliseconds. A large explosion. MAMs dead, flung about the desert earth. The class cheers.

"Today we'll be discussing the law of war."

Sometimes it's an AH-1W Super Cobra. An attack helicopter mounted with a 20 mm Gatling gun. Its loud whir gives warning to a group of MAMs trying to make a run for it. They "squirt." Run off in every direction. The pilot gives pursuit. Multiple round bursts trace their way onto the targets until every last one of them is dead. Lifeless. A few more rounds are fired off for good measure.

The class roars.

"Today's period of instruction is close air support."

It's like watching our favorite football team score another touchdown. We never really know what's going on in these video clips. A pilot somewhere engages a target and destroys it. Syria, Iraq, Afghanistan, Yemen, Somalia. Some place with desert. We never know. We never know the full story.

I'm dreaming. I'm thinking. I'm remembering.

I remember the first time I met Jay. He showed me this video on YouTube. It opens to the sound of gunfire echoing off concrete walls. It's the familiar snap, crackle, and pop of American five-five-six.

Inaccurate seven-six-two thuds, its rounds crashing just short of the cameraman's on-screen subjects, peppering them with dirt, rocks, adrenaline.

139

Center screen.

A group of soldiers huddled behind a brick wall. One of them fires his M-4.

Snap-snap-snap.

The others just sit there. They seem relaxed leaning there against the wall. One of them calmly shouts into a green radio. A building just out of view implodes. The sky is blue, and the sun shines brightly. Soldiers on screen smile. Palm trees dot the background.

Jay says to me "I took that video. Fucking good times man."

He wears an Aloha shirt, billabong board shorts, and a pair of Reef sandals. Oakley sunglasses atop his greasy black hair. He is short and stocky with a perpetual five o'clock shadow beard. I meet Jay after my first deployment.

Two weeks of leave after nine months overseas. I'm moving into a new loft in downtown Honolulu. Jay introduces himself to me while the landlord shows me around the building.

"You Marine?" he asks

"Yeah, you?"

"Was a medic in Iraq and Afghanistan."

The landlord apologizes. She asks him to leave. I say it's okay. Jay offers to help me move in. We click right away.

I soon find out that Jay is the real deal. A retired Army Ranger with real combat experience. He likes to tell stories. I like to listen.

Jay also likes to read, and he likes to talk about the ancient Greeks, and the "History of the Peloponnesian War," and he likes to quote Thucydides, and sip whiskey straight from a plastic cup, and smoke cigars nonstop.

And while I am on leave, Jay and I hang out at the bar downtown. Every night we go out to meet women. Every night some new woman falls in love with his stories. He is loud, boisterous, and confident. He is rude, and he is mean.

At first he says really sweet things to the women we meet. He says hello, and offers compliments. And as he drinks more, he gives more compliments. Until he drinks so much he erupts. Out bursts a stream of expletives. His victim breaks down into tears and frantically runs away fearing for her own safety. His language is offensive, indecent, vulgar. "Look at that fucking cunt," he says.

Jay likes to make people cry. And he likes to laugh when he sees how he's hurt people. And he likes to watch YouTube videos showing bombs destroying buildings, and crew-served weapons collapsing walls. And explosions. And death. And the pain associated with powerful loss that can be derived only from a hate so deep, it is otherworldly and mystical.

Jay enjoys harming innocent people unprovoked. It is something familiar to him.

I soon begin to distance myself from Jay. Over the course of one week, I realize Jay needs a kind of help I am incapable of providing. He is dangerous. He is to be avoided.

Jay knows this before I do. And he is in pain. And you know his deployments are a cause of pain to him. And his life is a life riddled by an undiagnosed PTSD. And as far as I am concerned, I am just a stranger. But Jay does not see it that way. I am his friend. I am supposed to help him.

Jay has a fiancée who is divorced. She lives with her 13-year-old daughter in a ground-floor apartment up on the hills overlooking Waikiki. Her name is Alicia. I meet her one morning when she drops by for breakfast with Jay. I introduce myself to her.

"She can help him," I think. I am wrong. She can't.

Jay met Alicia through Alcoholics Anonymous. Against the rules, and their better judgment, they decided to date. Later, they were engaged. She tells me this with a nervous grin. Something's wrong. I am not quite sure what it is.

I'm not sure Alicia is ready to marry Jay. But it is none of my business and I try to stay out of it. But Jay won't leave me alone.

He starts to come over to my apartment every day with something new. A bookshelf. A table. A new chair. Some pots and dishes. A book that "you have to read," he says. Later, a stack of books and DVDs that "you have to check out, man."

Jay starts to come over to just leave stuff in my apartment. And I think he is crazy for shedding all his belongings.

One day, he gives me a business card. On it is the name of a Navy Lieutenant Commander. Jay tells me I should give the guy a call. He says this guy is a former mentor of his. The Lieutenant Commander is "someone nice to know," he says. I throw the card away. I don't understand what it is Jay is trying to tell me.

Fourteen days go by. I check in off leave. I start locking my door, and ignoring Jay. I report back to duty. And then it happens.

I hear from my landlord that Jay broke up with Alicia. And for a few days, I don't hear anything from him. I don't look for him. In fact, I sigh with relief. "Our short friendship is over," I think. I'm wrong. Things are far from over.

Jay knocks on my door. I ignore it. The knocks become louder. I crack the door, he bursts in. He is clutching a pistol in his right hand. He is animated. He has a cigar in his mouth.

My friend Phil and I both look at each other. We ready ourselves to tackle Jay. With his eyes, Phil asks if this is the guy I told him about. I nod.

Jay picks up on this. He racks the slide back to show us the pistol's empty chamber and magazine weld. Clouds of light gray smoke billow up inside the apartment. He asks us if we have any ammunition.

None of this makes any sense to either of us. Jay stares at me impatiently. We can tell he is plotting something. Phil and I are alert.

He asks for a ride. We say no. He leaves. I lock the door. It is close to midnight.

Today, we're getting a series of briefs on targeting. It's part of our mandatory pre-deployment training. Distinction. Collateral damage. Target nomination. Verification. Another video. A building implodes.

My phone rings. It's my landlord. "Have you seen Jay recently?" she asks.

"Yeah, he came over last night. Why?"

"Jay's dead." Everything around me goes silent. I'm dizzy.

She goes on. "Just after midnight last night, Jay went over to Alicia's. He killed her, her daughter, and their dog. Then he killed himself."

I am in the classroom. Cheers. Another building collapses. I see Jay smiling, showing me that video he took.

THE CORNER OF MY HEART

Victoria Sylvander

I am 10 years old. My fifth-grade teacher is cautioning the class about a sex scene in a novel about prehistoric humans; we will have to get parental permission if we want to read the book.

My parents have had to tell me what sex is three times; the first two times, I found the idea so irrelevant to my life that I quickly forgot what sex was even called. So, I raise my hand and ask my teacher how prehistoric humans knew to have sex, because if they hadn't figured that out, how would the species have continued? My teacher hesitates before coming up with an answer: "instinct."

I nod, still not understanding, but not wanting to lose my reputation as the class brain by admitting I have no idea what he is talking about. Somewhere, in a small corner of my heart, I know that I do not and never will have this "instinct." This idea is unsettling. I put it out of my mind.

I am 11 years old. I am aware that men and women date and marry later in their lives, and the age when dating begins happening is rapidly approaching. I am also aware that I have no interest in dating or marrying a man.

At lunch, a boy accuses me of "liking" a friend of his who bullies me. I don't understand that this is only to get a rise out of me, and a rise it gets: I holler at him, "I don't even like boys!"

His rejoinder: "So are you gay?"

I am only vaguely aware of the concept of gayness. As far as I know, gay men are not interested in women, and gay women are not interested in men. I assume that this means a gay person is attracted to no one. I think this might be me. I shoot back, honestly, "Maybe!"

The boy immediately tells his friends that I'm gay. I recognize his tone as mocking. I understand that there is something wrong with being gay.

I am 12 years old. I am in a sex education class for the first time. My school ascribes to abstinence-only sex education at this age, saying we should not have sex until we are married and ready for children. The idea of having sex makes my skin crawl in repulsion. I am relieved that if I want to avoid it, all I have to do is not marry. I feel safe in that knowledge.

I am 13 years old. I am about to attend a school dance. I have been to dances before. I have seen boys and girls dancing together, and I have seen the boys hold their dance partners by the butt. I assure my mother that any boy who tries that with me will be met with violence, and that I will never want a boy to touch me that way.

My mother tries to convince me that my attitude is wrong; one day, I will want a boy touching me. A voice from the corner of my heart, tiny but fierce, whispers, "no."

I am 14 years old, a freshman in high school, and I am receiving sex education again. I have also read several books on puberty and dating. I learn that boys have a higher sex drive than girls. I feel vindicated in my knowledge that if a boy gropes me, it is acceptable for me to become violent; I would only be defending myself.

My feeling of vindication doesn't last when I learn that there are ways to have "safe" sex before marriage. I do not understand the idea of "safe" sex. To me, sex is always violent and not wanted. I am told that everyone wants and has sex, and I realize I will not be protected from sex by never marrying.

I realize this means that I do not want sex, but will be subjected to it anyway, and I want to crawl into the corner of my heart where I am safe, hide there forever, because I now know I can expect to be raped at some point in my life.

I am 15 years old. I am on the lacrosse team. My teammates are discussing which boys are cute and which boys they're interested in. I say nothing. One of my teammates asks me, "So, who do you like?" I stammer out that I don't like boys yet, though I think that crushes might happen at some point. (I don't know if I believe this; it is something others have told me. It is easier to explain than the truth.) My teammate's mouth drops open and she cries, "You don't like boys yet? That's so sad! So much of high school is dating!"

For the rest of the lacrosse season, my teammates try to teach me how to like boys. They point out which male actors, singers, and classmates are "cute." I never say anything in response.

I am 16 years old. I am on a date with a boy. I do not want to be here. I have told myself that I will develop sexual feelings for this boy if I date him. I think my life would be easier if I were sexually attracted to boys. It would mean that when sex inevitably happened to me, it wouldn't be rape.

The boy kisses me. The corner of my heart is screaming "no," but I tell myself not to listen. My stomach roils in revulsion. Later, I will learn terms like "heteronormativity" and "consent" that will help explain this situation, but at the time, the only word I have for the kiss is "wrong."

Trying not to let my face betray my disgust, I lean back. The boy looks at me like I am a cut of meat he wants to devour. I give up on forcing myself to be heterosexual.

I am 17 years old, and some days, I have the world figured out: women do not experience sexual attraction. They only submit to sex to appease male partners, because society has brainwashed them into believing they want sex, or because they want children. My friends who have had crushes on boys or who have had sex are, sadly, brainwashed. Men, however, experience sexual attraction; someone has to, or the species would die out. Because of this, men are dangerous. I don't want them looking at me. I don't want them anywhere near me.

When I listen to my AP biology teacher talk about human sexuality, I roll my eyes, thinking myself more enlightened than my classmates, who believe her lies. The answer has to be that women who don't experience sexual attraction are normal. Human. I have to be a normal human. I have to be.

On other days, I accept my defectiveness. I accept that crushes are normal for women and that I am not normal. I jokingly call myself a "biological snafu," but I laugh because that is the alternative to crying because I am not human. On these days, I understand that I am a flawed product that deserves only to be discarded, and to endure the pain with a determined grimace as I draw scissor blades across my skin.

I am 18 years old. I am seated in front of my computer. I have bolted from an event held in my dorm: a talk about women's sexuality. I had chosen to attend wondering if I would hear something that would help me understand myself, but was driven away by a graphic description; I'm surprised I didn't vomit on the spot. I had certainly felt sick enough.

There has to be a reason I find sex so frightening, so repugnant. Something about me that is not unique to me. I do something I should have done years ago: enter "asexuality in humans" into a search engine.

I find a site dedicated to asexual visibility and education. Everything is there. Everything. Definitions. Descriptions. Frequently asked questions. Testimonials from asexual people.

There's a word for it. There's a word for it. There's a word for it.

I am not a "biological snafu." I am not subhuman. I am not broken.

I am asexual.

My cheeks are damp and I'm not sure how they got that way. The corner of my heart sings.

I am still 18, and I have a crush on a woman for a first time. I have learned that it is possible for asexual people to experience romantic feelings. It has taken me a few months to pry the entwined ideas of sex and romance apart in my brain, but I understand that I am experiencing a crush. (The jury remains deadlocked over whether or not I had crushes on women when I was younger.) I do not want sex with my crush, but I want just about everything else: time spent watching YouTube videos in her room, chatting over Thai food, braiding her hair.

Sometimes I think about kissing her.

When I tell her that I am starting a club for asexual people and allies on our college campus, she tells me she has experienced plenty of sexual feelings, but never romantic feelings. I never tell her about my crush on her.

I am 19 years old, watching a science fiction show I love with a woman I have fallen hard for, and we kiss. It feels good. It feels right. (It helps that she's a good kisser.)

Later, though the corner of my heart is overjoyed that I have found someone, some darker part of me is disappointed. It was expecting to feel a stirring in my groin during that kiss, something that would unbreak me, something that would finally make me want sex, make me human.

I am 20 years old, and I have had sex for the first time, with the woman I kissed when I was 19. It was loving, and consensual. I am still not sexually attracted to her, but I wanted to make her feel good. I am pleased (and somewhat relieved) to discover that my repulsion evaporates when I am emotionally comfortable with someone. I will sleep well next to my lover, and will always look back fondly on this night.

I have heard a seemingly infinite number of people insist that I can't know I am asexual until I have had sex. Well, I have had sex, and I'm still asexual. The corner of my heart snickers, once: "ha."

I am still 20 years old. I am at a pride parade for the first time. I am wearing a shirt that reads "asexual: a person who does not experience sexual attraction" on the back. I feel a tap on my shoulder; it's a white cis gay man who tells me that my shirt has the definition of "asexual" wrong. I insist that I am asexual, that my shirt bears a definition agreed on by thousands of asexual people, and that he doesn't know what he is talking about.

He insists that he is a psychologist, so he knows that "asexual" means "not experiencing arousal." I want to snap that I stopped seeing my last therapist because she was wrong about asexuality too, but incoherent rage knocks the words from my mind.

I am 21 years old, and I am experiencing heartbreak, the kind of heartbreak that makes you hurt so badly that you look in the mirror and are surprised to not see a blooded hole blown though your chest, for the first time. Though I am a junior, I am staying on my college campus after the school year is over; I am helping with graduation. At the commencement ceremony, I hug my ex-lover and tell her I'm proud of her.

I expect that this will be the last time I see her. I am planning to end my own life over the summer. I have discovered that I have a need for romantic love. And now I have lost the only person who could ever look past my asexuality enough to love me. I am planning to wait a few months, so she doesn't think it's because of the breakup. But I don't expect to see my senior year of college.

I am still 21 years old, starting my final year of college by the grace of antidepressants, a decent therapist, and the continued friendship of my ex-lover. I have attempted to take my asexual visibility efforts further than my campus with a YouTube series.

It's YouTube. I get nothing but negative comments. "Your mama must have dropped you on your head when you were a baby" is one of the tamer ones. Another person, attempting to be helpful, tells me that it's fine if I want a relationship with a "normal" person as long as I'm okay with polyamory; being asexual, I could never be enough of a romantic partner all on my own. (It is not until later that I understand how unfair this was to both polyamory and me.)

The corner of my heart aches like a bruise. I am sure that if I could look at it, it would be purpled and misshapen. I don't know how to heal it.

I am 22 years old. I am dating another asexual woman. We cosplay as Harley Quinn and Poison Ivy for a convention. Another attendee tells me that since we are both asexual, we shouldn't be dressed as those characters; Harley and Ivy are "highly sexual." He goes on to insist that asexuality is a choice. I don't remember what I said to him. But I remember it was not said so much as shouted.

I am 23 years old. I am a college graduate, now working in a public library. In the young adult section, I spy a young adult book about sexuality, including queer sexuality. I page through it hungrily, expecting to find, at the very least, a definition of asexuality. There is nothing.

The battered corner of my heart cries out. I feel sickened and angry and invisible to the world as my hands type out an email to the author, insisting that representing asexuality is important, giving the example of how I feel at the moment. She replies saying she admires my passion, but that her book is about sex, so there is no need to mention asexuality.

It's too much. The door to the corner of my heart swings closed and locks with an almost audible click.

I am 27 years old. It has been four years since I visited an asexuality website or produced a video on asexuality. I attended a pride parade a few months ago, where I wore the colors of the asexual pride flag, but had focused mostly on draping myself in rainbows and hoping no one noticed the purple, black, and gray color scheme I also wore. I don't think about how this hope clashes horribly with the fact that, several years ago, I helped design the asexual flag.

I am listening to an instrumental track composed by the guitarist of my rock band. As I mentally search for a lyrical topic, the music unlocks the corner of my heart that I have neglected. Its door swings open. My fingers fly over the keyboard, words pouring out of me, and I have a chorus within a few minutes:

It seemed easier to stay inside
To choose safety over pride
But I will claim my identity
To help others who are like me

I name the song "Pride." I sing it at rehearsal, and the drummer asks me what the lyrics are about. Willing my voice not to shake, I tell him it is about my being asexual. I know he is a therapist. I expect to hear phrases like "medication side effect" and "female sexual interest disorder." I expect to hear something that will make me quit the band on the spot. Instead, he says he is aware there is a "whole community" of people who identify as asexual, and he knows some of them. The guitarist says the same.

I relax, but I am stunned. I can't believe that just happened.

I am still 27 years old. I am perusing writing contests, looking for a few to enter. I find one that requests submission of "stories that need to be told." I think about that phrase: "stories that need to be told."

I am 26, being told I'm not queer enough because I'm asexual. I am 22, being told I should expect any romantic partner to cheat on me because they wouldn't be able to stand my not being sexually attracted to them. I am 20, being told I am only asexual because I am autistic. I am 18, crying in the resource center for sexuality and gender at my college because it has no resources on asexuality. I am 13, being told I'm being immature because I find sex disgusting and frightening. I am 11, knowing something there is horribly, incorrigibly wrong with me.

I am 27 again, and the rush of memories churns my brain and my stomach. I am on my knees in front of the toilet. Stomach acid burns my throat, the inside of my nose.

I rinse my mouth, return to my computer, and open a word processing program. I write this. It comes straight from the corner of my heart.

POBRECITO

Nina Joy Silver

It was a sunny fall day in the outdoor market in Mexico City. The aromas of roasting chili peppers, fresh coffee beans grinding, wood burning on a corner to warm a vendor, and fresh cut flowers mingled in the crisp, cool air. I could hear the sounds of the tortilla ladies pit-patting as they formed tortillas in the palms of their hands, then throwing them onto a little wood-burning stove to brown each side, crying out: "¿Tortillas, Señora?" competing with each other to sell their wares. The balloon man's whistle. A donkey braying. There were street musicians: a father and two sons who played the xylophone on the corner. And, of course, the sight of Popo and Itzy; the two snow-capped volcanoes stood clear on the horizon watching over Mexico City and my market. The year was 1955 and I was 11 years old.

My mother and I had just stepped out of our ultramodern high-rise building into the fresh-air market. We lived in the penthouse, a beautiful apartment with a panoramic view of Mexico City, high above the chaos of the market where the poor tried to make a living and beggars begged. My mother was in her usual attire: high heels, nylons, skirt, and blouse and a pocket book hanging from her arm, ready to go food shopping. She was happy, so I was too. It was going to be a good day.

Suddenly we heard a scream and the sound of glass breaking. Someone yelled, "Ay, pobrecito!" (Oh poor thing!) Two "pobrecitos" (little poor boys) about eight and nine years old wearing dark cotton overalls that were too wide and too short, no shirts, and no shoes, were about ten feet from where we were. A crowd formed to see what had happened. We caught a glimpse of the smaller pobrecito between people's legs and heard him cry, "Ay, Mamá!" We headed toward the

151

boy since we had to go in that direction to get to the center of the market. As we approached I heard somebody say, "Ahí viene La Enojona" (Here comes the angry/mad woman). I flinched. My mother had a reputation. She would get into verbal fights with people but only on the days she wasn't being incredibly sweet. It didn't happen often in public, but when it did, it was embarrassing for me. Luckily she didn't hear the comment. She wouldn't have understood anyway. She spoke very little Spanish.

When we got to the boy we could see blood on the sidewalk near a broken glass bottle. We stopped walking and froze. A terrible gash in the fleshy part of his hand between the thumb and the forefinger was bleeding profusely. He was on his knees, crying, holding his arm straight out and down.

"Hold your arm down! Hold your arm down!" his frightened friend was screaming at him. The blood ran onto the sidewalk.

In the busy marketplace, several people stopped and looked, shook their heads, tsked, tsked and said, "Pobrecito, pobrecito," and kept right on walking. Nobody was going to help him.

My mother thrust her pocket book into my arms and flew to him. She grabbed his arm and held it straight up to stop the flow of blood.

"Tell him to come with us," she said, using me as translator. "Tell him I will help him and not to be afraid." All she could say was "Pobrecito, pobrecito," (poor little boy) over and over again. He slowly stared up at her in shock. His friend ran off.

The crowd in the marketplace watched in dismay as this crazy American woman did what they considered unthinkable. Never letting go and holding his arm straight up, she led him into our building and into the elevator. He stopped sobbing. Now he was in awe. His eyes popped. It was obvious he had never been in such a building. We walked across the highly polished, pink marble floor of the lobby toward the elevator. He turned his head from side to side and up and down. He was looking at everything. I was looking at him. He saw himself reflected over and over in the mirrored walls. It looked like there were 100 barefoot pobrecitos wearing the same overalls in my lobby.

In the elevator his huge dark eyes got even bigger. He was at the gulping air, shuddering, quiet stage of crying. The tears cut a path through the chalky white dust on his cinnamon cheeks.

"Pobrecito," my mother said so soothingly, still holding his arm straight up as we rode to the top floor of our building. She stood with him in the back corner of the elevator. I stood with my back to the elevator door, facing him. "No tengas miedo." I said so softly, "Don't be afraid." I felt I should speak very quietly, he was that scared.

We went into our apartment and into the bathroom. I got a thick book for him to stand on so he could reach the sink. He jumped when the water was turned on. I don't think he had ever seen plumbing. My mother cleaned his hand ever so gently. She poured peroxide over it and did a professional job of bandaging it with sterile gauze pads and gauze bandage that wrapped around the hand and wrist.

"Ask him if he has a mamá," she said.

"¿Tienes un mamá?" I asked.

He did have a mamá. She lived in a village just outside the city.

"Ask him if there's a doctor in his village."

"¿Hay un doctor ahí?"

Yes, there was a "clinica." We told him he must go straight home to his mamá and that he must go to the clinic because it wasn't enough to bandage the cut, it needed more attention. In the meantime it was clean and the bleeding had stopped. We told him he had to keep it clean and dry and not to touch the bandages, to let a doctor do it.

My mother led him to the kitchen and told the maids to prepare food and drink for him and his friend. They had a long walk home ahead of them. He had said his friend would find him as soon as he went outside. The maids wouldn't let him in the kitchen.

"¡No! ¡Fuchí! ¡Súcio! He's too dirty for 'our' kitchen!"

I saw that they were afraid of what they might catch. They covered their noses and mouths. They didn´t want to breathe any air that he exhaled. I was glad they didn't let him see or hear how they were acting.

"Niño, ëspérate aquí" (Child, wait here). They shooed him outside the back door of the kitchen onto the fire escape while they packed two sandwiches and drinks for him to take and handed the package to him.

"Gracias," he said. He wouldn't take the elevator down. He took the stairs.

I wondered what he thought about the whole experience. I imagined him telling his mamá and the doctor at the clinic: "¡Una Señora Americana!"

I was proud of my enojona mother for a moment, but I didn't dwell on it. I went on with my life of school and friends. The incident was just about forgotten.

One afternoon a month later the doorbell rang. My mother wasn't home, the maids were busy, so I opened the door. For a moment I didn't recognize the pobrecito. He had grown and he was scrubbed, squeaky clean, and was all dressed up in bleached white cotton pants with a rope around the waist holding them up, a bleached white shirt, straw sombrero on his head with shiny black hair peeking out, and this time, sandals on his clean feet. Cupped in his hands was a little potted cactus plant with one blossom on it. He held it up and said, "Mi mamá quiere que tu mamá tenga esto." And he handed it to me.

"¡Que lindo! ¡Gracias!" I said. Our eyes met and we just smiled at each other for a good 10 seconds, then he turned and ran down the stairs.

"How brave of his mamá to do this! And my mother too!! How good!"

I couldn't wipe the smile off my face for the rest of the afternoon.

The next morning I went out into the marketplace. The aroma of fresh coffee beans grinding began. The donkey brayed. The tortilla ladies pit-patted. The balloon man blew his whistle. The xylophone family filled the air with music. The scent of fresh cut flowers mingled with the aroma of chili peppers roasting.

LOVERS' LAST JOURNEY

Bob Blake

The wicked clot had stolen almost everything
My speech, my movement, my freedom
But not—in those final moments—
My treasure trove of memories
The world beckoned, and we answered

We found our Shangri-La
At the farthest end of the Great Wall
Gazed, in awe, atop a Dragon's Backbone
Strolled hand-in-hand through a forest made of stone
Our life together, a splendid mandala

Go toward the light, my love.

In a land of 30,000 gods
We rode elephants through a forest of majestic tigers
Searched the Pink City for lost temples
Our suite adorned with Kama Sutra that made us blush
Our life together, a feast for the eyes

Go toward the light, my love.

Enchanted by street tango in La Boca
We indulged in the most fantastic bottle of Malbec
Danced steamy nights away in a hidden milonga
All sweat and salsa, like Latin Lovers
Our life together, a boldly painted mural

Go toward the light, my love.

We found our Pura Vida in a shack beside the Pacific
Snapped racy Polaroids only we could see
Rode donkeys down the volcano on a dare
Stumbled upon orchids that smelled of chocolate
Our life together, a delicious mystery

Go toward the light, my love.

With my last breath I took her back to where it all began
The waterfront in Charleston
The ring, down on one knee, tears coursing her cheeks
She was the seven wonders of my world
To love, to honor, to wander
Etched in our vows

Go toward the light, my love.

The allure of the light, so blindingly bright
Now I can embrace it